MICHIGAN
TRAILMAKERS

A SECTION OF OAKLAND COUNTY MICHIGAN

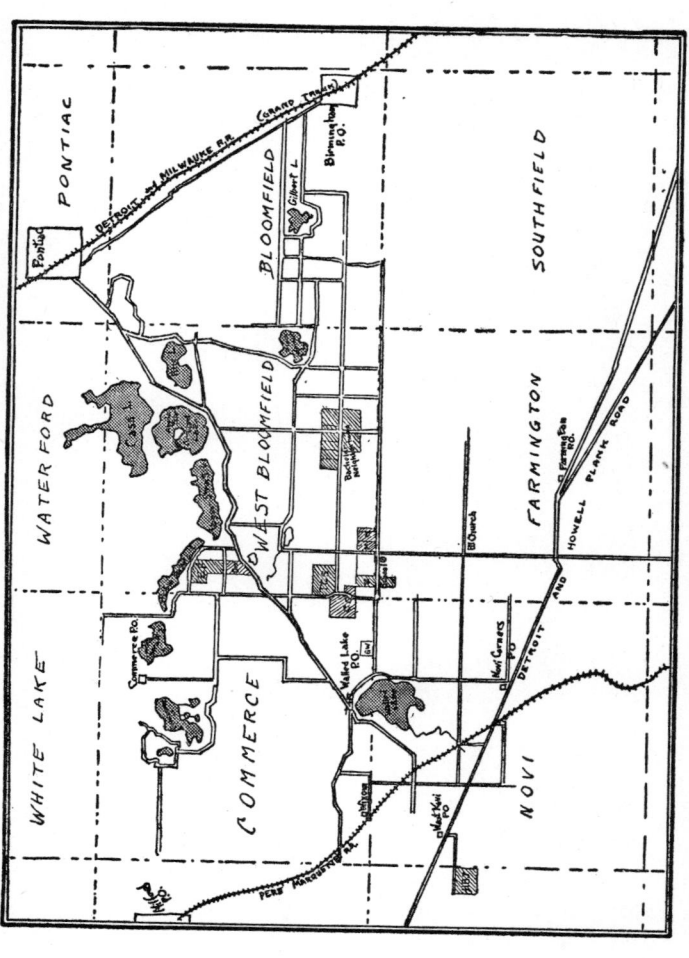

MICHIGAN TRAILMAKERS

BY

HENRY ORMAL SEVERANCE, Litt. D.,
LIBRARIAN
UNIVERSITY OF MISSOURI

Author of "History of the Library—
University of Missouri."

FOREWORD
by
FREDERICK BLACKMAR MUMFORD,
Dean of the Faculty of Agriculture,
University of Missouri

ANN ARBOR
GEORGE WAHR, Publisher
1930

Copyright 1930
By GEORGE WAHR

MADE IN U.S.A.

FRANKLIN DeKLEINE COMPANY
PRINTERS AND BINDERS
LANSING, MICHIGAN

DEDICATION

THIS WORK IS DEDICATED TO THE MEMORY OF THE PIONEERS AND TRAILMAKERS WHOSE LIVES AND DEEDS HAVE HELPED TO MAKE MICHIGAN A GREAT STATE.

FOREWORD

THE historian who can accurately record the ideals, ambitions, and achievements of the pioneers is rendering a distinct public service. The second and third generations following the original settlers have builded upon the character foundations of the pioneers. The remarkable development of the United States and the sweep of its population from the Atlantic to the Pacific is one of the most romantic and moving pages in all history. The fundamental causes of the peaceful occupation of a continent are to be found in the rugged characters, integrity and tireless industry of a pioneer race.

The author of "Michigan Trailmakers" has made a real contribution to our knowledge of this era. The account is the more valuable in that it places before us the intimate, daily lives of the early settlers. Their enthusiasms, their labors, their pleasures, their devotion to religious ideals are very clearly recorded in this interesting record.

FREDERICK BLACKMAR MUMFORD,

Dean of the faculty of Agriculture, and Director of the Agricultural Experiment Station, University of Missouri.

PREFACE

THE purpose of this story is to put into permanent form a picture of the early settlement of southern Michigan, particularly the section embraced in the limits of Oakland County. Charles is a representative of this period and section. The story of his settling in Commerce township, the clearing of the land, the erection of the log house and barns, the raising of crops with primitive tools such as the cradle, scythe and the three cornered harrow, are typical of all the others. The story includes an account of how the early settlers lived, what they ate and what they wore, the rearing of children, the organization of the district schools and the church relations and the social activities such as sports and games and "bees," courtship, marriage and the like.

After the settlers became established on their farms, they gave attention to fertilization of their soil; the use of new and improved machinery; the importation and breeding of the best grades of live stock.

In the later period Charles L. is the representative farmer and villager. "We are and should be interested in how any man solves his problems and acquits himself in his battles" wrote F. L. Mott in his *Rewards of Reading*. He was one of the thousands of farmers who, after the Civil War, trekked west over the western frontiers and made homes on the prairies. They went with little or no capital, with few tools and without comforts, built log and sod houses, cleared and cultivated large acreages. They were subject to conditions and circumstances over which, individually, they had no control. The enormous over-production of wheat and other grains from 1868 to 1873 forced prices to such low levels that hundreds of farmers couldn't pay their taxes and interest on their mortgages. The result was that farmers were sold out for the face of the mortgages, losing all their improvements and buildings. Many of them faced about, trekked back east as Charles L. did.

Then followed the organization of farmers into alliances, granges and Patrons of Husbandry—for their better protection against the predatory interests of the country.

The sources of information for this work are: books, especially the collection of the *Michigan Pioneer and Historical Society;* men and women whose lives spanned the period of 1835 to date and from my personal recollections. Much information was obtained from Charles L. and Louisa and her brother Edwin Forbush before their decease; from the daughter of Wells Hartsough, still living, now in her ninety-third year; from Elisha Farmer, nearly ninety years of age who married Lavancha, daughter of Edwin Forbush; and Mrs. Jane Ann Power, daughter of Samuel Bachelor, born and reared in the Bachelor neighborhood, now in her eighty-ninth year.

H. O. SEVERANCE.

November 26, 1929.

CONTENTS

CHAPTER		PAGE
I.	LURE OF THE WEST	1
II.	THE WESTWARD JOURNEY	9
III.	FIRST WINTER IN MICHIGAN 1835-36	21
IV.	THE NEW HOME IN COMMERCE TOWNSHIP	32
V.	LIFE IN THE WOODS	40
VI.	CHARLES L.	56
VII.	THE FORBUSHES	72
VIII.	CHARLES L. WINS A BRIDE	82
IX.	ISAAC LAMB AND HIS KNITTING MACHINE	99
X.	SAINT JOHNS	106
XI.	THE ILLINOIS FARM	114
XII.	VILLAGE LIFE—WALLED LAKE	134
	BIBLIOGRAPHY	153
	INDEX	157

ILLUSTRATIONS

MAP. SECTION OF OAKLAND CO.
MAP. ANDALUSIA TOWNSHIP.

MICHIGAN
TRAILMAKERS

MICHIGAN TRAILMAKERS

CHAPTER I

LURE OF THE WEST

THE early settlers of Michigan came largely from New York, New England, and Pennsylvania. The East was becoming overcrowded; Michigan was virgin territory where land could be purchased from the government at $1.00 an acre in 1817 and $1.25 an acre later. At the close of the War of 1812, Congress set aside six million acres for homesteads for the American soldiers who fought in that war with Great Britain of which two million acres were to be located in Michigan. The Surveyor-General came out from Washington to make surveys and locate the land for the soldiers. He and his staff evidently set out from Detroit, where the land was low and marshes abundant, and made their way into Oakland County,—the County of lakes and marshes—or they may have gone north into Michigan from Toledo and passed over the marshy lands of northeastern Ohio and southeastern Michigan. The marshes appeared to be lakes with a heavy sod of marsh grass over the water. Marshes were springy like thin ice. When one walked over them one's foot would sink down and the sod would bulge up on all sides. The process would be repeated with every step. The timber and underbrush indicated low swampy land full of mosquitoes and ague. The Surveyor knew that the willows, poplars, cedars, and tamaracks grew in low places, so that the Surveyor without penetrating far into the interior, reported to the authorities in Washington that: "Taking the country altogether, so far as has been explored, and to all appearances, together with information received concerning the balance, is so bad there would not be more than one acre out of a hundred, if there should be one out of a thousand, that would in any case admit of cultivation."

In the light of this report the government abandoned its plan of assigning two million acres of land for soldiers' homesteads in Michigan. The unfavorable condition of Michigan for settlement as indicated by this report was published in the Eastern papers. The overcrowded East which was looking west for opportunities to settle and make homes for itself would not consider the marshy wilderness of Michigan for future homes. The home seekers settled in Ohio, Indiana and Illinois instead of in Michigan. There was no inducement for farmers, eking out a bare existence on the stony hills of New England, to sell out and move west to the marshlands of Michigan. A few adventurers, like Thomas Palmer and his brother, Friend, itinerant merchants from Canandaigua, New York, came soon after the War of 1812 and opened a grocery and general merchandise store in Detroit; and a few trail blazers, like John Graham, Christopher Hartsough and John

Hersey, settled in Oakland County, March 17, 1817; other pioneers who braved the dangers of the marshes, mud holes and lakes described in the Surveyor's report, explored the county, found dry land, oak openings, hills, valleys, and wooded lands, and settled there and wrote to their kinfolk and friends in the east urging them to come west to the "promised land". They wrote in the highest praise of their new country. Many of the prospectors and explorers went back to New York to get their families. They spread the news about Michigan and urged their friends to pull up and go west. By 1820 there were five hundred people in Oakland County alone. Immigrants continued to come in large numbers so that this county contained five thousand population by 1830.

Missionaries followed the pioneer settlers. The church in the East felt that the early settlers, of all classes of people, would need the encouragement, consolation and inspiration of the ministers of the Gospel. The Baptist Missionary Convention of New York, organized in 1821, sent Reverend Elkanah Comstock as missionary to Wayne, Oakland and Washtenaw counties in 1822; and Reverend Nehemiah Lamb in 1824 who was accompanied by his two sons, Caleb and Aroswill. Nehemiah returned to New York but settled permanently in Michigan in 1830. These ministers wrote home and to friends and at times visited the kinfolk in the east, and told them of this wonderful country. Caleb returned to New York after a month in Michigan and by word of mouth spread the news and said that he would return to Michigan to live as soon as he could save enough money to pay his moving expenses. One of his sisters married Horace Johns of Genessee County, New York. The Johnses moved to Michigan in 1825 and were pioneer settlers near Novi, Oakland County; another sister, Martha, married Charles Severance of Washington, New Hampshire, in 1830; and Susan married his brother, Ezra, later. The girls were obsessed with the idea of making trails into Michigan. Their father and mother and two brothers had already moved their household goods to Michigan and made their homes there. In the meantime, Charles and Ezra had become discontented with farming on the hills of New Hampshire. They felt the general discontent among farmers. The urge to emigrate, take up land and to make homes in Michigan finally overcame the inertia of a century and they did move.

Charles' great-grandfather, Daniel, had settled on a little farm in the valley of the Ashuelot River which drained the waters from a small lake where the little hamlet of Washington was situated and carried them into the Connecticut River. His father, Benjamin, was descended from that well-known ancestor John Severans of Salisbury, Massachusetts, who came to Boston in 1637 from Ipswich, England. He married Betsy Dodge of Andover, Vermont, had lived here to the end of his days and so did several uncles. There was a little colony of them. Charles was born here in 1805 and after him, seven brothers and three sisters. The Severances, like most New Englanders, believed in large families, especially large families of boys, as they helped to earn a living for the family. The boys worked out from the age of nine or ten until they were of age, 21, and gave all their earnings to their parents to help defray the expenses of the family. Boys of nine years of age who could drive an ox team and do chores were hired at $1.00 a week and board. This rate, of course, was increased as the boy matured, grew stronger and more efficient. The boys had to get up at sunrise and feed the oxen then came the simple breakfast. Charles would yoke the oxen and perhaps plow some corn ground, striking his bare feet against the stones, which were already sore with "stone bruises." In haying and harvest, he drove the oxen and two wheeled cart which the farmer would pile high with hay or grain, and woe to the boy if his carelessness in driving over the side hill would cause the cart to tip over. He would have been scolded and might have been sent to bed without his supper. After supper came the chores, care of the oxen, of the cows, sheep, chickens, and filling the wood box. Then it was dark and bedtime.

Charles worked all summer and went to school three months in the winter. He enjoyed the swims in the summer, coasting and sledding on the ice, skiing, and "fox and geese" in the winter. The great event of the year was the "protracted meetings" in the winter to which everybody went. Two hour sermons were usual. There was no Sunday afternoon problem with children. They went to church forenoon and afternoon. This little town of Washington was isolated—no railroad anywhere near, no telephones, no telegraph, but the Government distributed the mail.

Charles and Ezra had now reached their majority and were still working out to get money for their own affairs, and were seriously considering their future. Charles said to Ezra: "I'm going to western New York or to some other country where the stones aren't so thick and the hills aren't so steep, where I can raise wheat, corn, oats and hay and not have to work against so many odds as I do here."

Ezra: "Think of the good times we have here; the boys and girls we like so well; the fishing and swimming in the summer, and the winter sports."

Charles: "There is nothing here for a young man who has ambition to own a farm and make a living on it for a family. Look at Uncle Daniel, Uncle Reuben, and Uncle Nathan and tell me if you think farming is a success. You can raise sheep on these hills but as the saying runs "you have to sharpen their noses so's they can get the grass between the stones!"

Ezra: "What about Michigan for a location? I had a letter from Susan (Lamb) who said her father and brothers, Caleb and Aroswell, had been there. They said they were going back there to live."

Charles: "That's a long way into the wilderness. I would like to see them and find out about Michigan, but York State still has some good land. Ontario County has good orchards and vineyards around Geneva. A further inducement, Martha has kinfolk there."

Information is not available for tracing the movements of the two brothers for the next five years. Charles married Martha Lamb in 1830, Ezra married Susan somewhat later, both were daughters of Reverend Nehemiah Lamb and Hannah Palmer Lamb, whose sister, Thankful B., married Wells Hartsough who lived at Gorham, Ontario County, New York.

Charles and Martha in 1830 located at Geneva, Ontario County, New York, within a few miles of their Uncle Wells Hartsough. Charles Lamb Severance was born here, December 14, 1833. Martha's father was pastor of the Hopewell Church in the county ten or twelve years before Charles came here to live. The lure of the West was too great for them to remain long in Geneva or for Ezra and Susan to spend their days in New Hampshire. Nehemiah had already moved to Michigan. Caleb had saved enough for expense of moving and settled in Michigan as a missionary pastor in 1829. He drove his horse and light wagon to Buffalo, carrying his wife and two children and household furniture. He took passage on the schooner, Commerce, which landed the party safely at Detroit. Then he drove to Joseph Gilbert's, his father-in-law, in Bloomfield township, Oakland County, where the family remained about a year while Caleb was visiting various settlements holding meetings and organizing churches. His travels took him to Farmington, Novi, Northville, Plymouth, Ypsilanti, Walled Lake, Pontiac, St. Johns, Troy, Avon, and many other places. He became acquainted with the pioneers, knew their farms, and the lands not yet purchased from the government. He wrote Martha and Susan and Uncle Wells urging them to come on before all the good land had been taken. He wrote that Cousin Thomas Palmer was in business in Detroit, and brother Horace (Johns) on a good farm south of Wixom, "winters not so cold as they are in New York and New England, snow covers the ground for two or three months, long summers. Farmers raise good crops of wheat, corn, rye, oats. Why not own a good farm and have something to show for your hard work when you are old?"

CHAPTER II
THE WESTWARD JOURNEY

THE Erie Canal, in course of construction for several years, was opened for traffic in 1825 from Lake Erie to Schenectady, connecting the Lake with the Mohawk River and with New York City. By opening up a new method of travel toward the West, the canal was the greatest agency for abetting immigration into Michigan and Wisconsin. Travel from East to West continued to be made by stage coach over the Mohawk and Genessee turnpike, and by covered wagons and horses and oxen. The cross state railroads were not built until several years later. The stage coach made better time between Albany and Buffalo than the canal boats but the fares were higher. A majority of the emigrants were going into the new country to make homes and would need horses and oxen and wagons, tools and household goods which could be taken on the boats, or on the covered wagon which could be driven through. Consequently, many emigrants went over the Mohawk and Genessee turnpike to Buffalo where most of them took a steamer across Lake Erie to Detroit, others skirted the south side of Lake Erie and came into Michigan from the south.

The emigrants were not usually pressed for time but hard pressed for money which they knew they would need for the purchase of supplies and seed potatoes and seed wheat and the like in their wilderness homes. Consequently, they travelled the cheapest way, either overland in covered wagons, or on the canal boats of which there were two classes, the fast and the slow boats. The fast boats, called the "express boats" which were the forerunners of our modern lake steamers, furnished rooms and beds and board for their passengers, and travelled at the rate of four miles an hour. The "line boats" or slow boats moved at the rate of three miles an hour. Deck space for passengers was practically all the line boats furnished. Passengers furnished their own beds and their own meals. The passengers on the express boats, when they passed a liner, would look out their cabin windows and smile, and feel sorry for the poor emigrants who had to ride on the deck exposed to the hot sun and the rain or the cold winds and frosty weather, much as the passengers in a pullman commiserate the poor folk who have to ride in coaches on local trains. But the emigrant must make his small amount of money go as far as he can. He knew the inconvenience of travel on a slow canal boat would leave him more money to lessen the deprivations and inconveniences of accommodations in his forest home. The "line boat" was a low narrow barge with only one deck. The passengers could get off at stations and get bread and milk and other necessary provisions. "No one lacked a place to sleep and no one went hungry. The worst of the hardships for the women was the lack of privacy," but women managed to keep house on the boat with amazing skill. The slowness of travel was offset by the restfulness of the water ride and by the variety of beautiful scenery along the way. Charles and Martha in 1830 left Washington, New Hampshire, went overland west to Albany and on to Schenectady. Here they took a "line boat." They sat in chairs on the deck or walked about and usually went ashore at the port stops. On the trip west, they passed through the beautiful valleys of New York and saw many improved farms, acres of orchards, vineyards, dairy farms, attractive little towns, large wheat fields, corn fields, meadows, forests, and lakes. Charles and Martha left the boat at Lenox and went south to Geneva about ten miles away where her kinfolk had lived. They settled on a farm and there remained until 1833. While they were here Lewis and Charles Lamb were born and Martha's father and mother visited them before they left for their home in Michigan. Caleb, Martha's brother, had already settled in Michigan and had written back telling of the large influx of immigrants into Oakland County, of the beautiful lakes, the fruitful farms and the quality of the emigrants, the pious, energetic, strenuous, courageous men and women who were bound to succeed. He wrote: "soil is productive, churches and schoolhouses are to be built, roads to be opened and rendered passable. In short, everything is waiting for strong and willing hands to make Michigan a great and prosperous state." In a postscript, he added the following from the colored barber who cut his hair in Buffalo: "Some people thinks they are fools that go to Michigan, but 'tain't so; the smart ones go to Michigan and the fools stay back."

Wells and Thankful Hartsough caught the western fever, sold their little farm, packed up their belongings and loaded them into a covered wagon, left Gorham, took the Mohawk and Genessee turnpike to Buffalo, and then the trail around the southern side of Lake Erie, through Ohio to Michigan. Charles and Martha decided to follow the Hartsough's and build a home in Michigan. Ezra and Susan decided to leave the hills of New Hampshire and go with them to Michigan. They arrived in Geneva in the summer of 1835 coming by canal boat, the route and the conveyances used by Charles and Martha four years previously.

The men made a cover for the wagon for protection from the rain and the sun. Into the ox-drawn wagon, they loaded their few household goods, a crate containing a cock and five hens, a crate of young pigs, some flour, pork, a shot gun, rifle and powder horns, and started toward Buffalo a hundred miles away. The women and children rode most of the way, the men walked. They camped by the wayside at night, usually near a farm house so they could get water and milk. They followed the Mohawk and Genessee turnpike, fording creeks, circling around lakes, passing over hills and through valleys and swamps in the beautiful lake country of western New York. Sometimes Martha's courage would wane when she looked upon her baby boys and thought of the hardships of pioneer life and of living in a log house in the wilderness inhabited by wild animals and wild Indians. Arriving in Buffalo on the fifth day, they found the steamer Michigan about to sail the next day.

They booked passage for themselves, the covered wagon and the oxen. They were astonished to find five hundred other passengers on board, most of them bound for Michigan to found homes as they were intending to do; others were going farther west to Chicago, Wisconsin, Kansas, and some to California.

When the steamer Michigan backed out of port at Buffalo about four o'clock in the afternoon, the Severance party, tired and weary with the long journey over land, was seated on deck in the stern. The ship backed out into the lake, righted about, and put to sea. When towers and steeples of Buffalo and the forests on either side of the town appeared to be moving away, and growing dim and finally were out of sight, tears came to the eyes of Martha and Susan. They thought of homes in Washington and Geneva and their friends and kinfolk whom they might never see again. They all moved to chairs on the front of the deck so they might look forward and speculate on their future homes. They had fond anticipation of the pleasure of a reunion of the Lambs, the Palmers and the Hartsoughs and the Johnes. They made plans for locating farm land, for clearing the trees ready for planting next spring, for the construction of houses and barns. Lewis and Charles Lamb were cross and sleepy, Martha looked pale and weary. She said: "I hope to have a good sleep tonight." The lake was smooth all night. When they came on deck the next morning, they were buoyant and cheerful. The children mingled with others of their age and went hopping and skipping on the deck. They made acquaintance with other emigrants. Several families, all seeking homes in Michigan were drawn into friendly visiting with the Severances, among whom were Colonel William Phelps who had not decided where he would locate, Sam Beery, wife and two boys from Chautauqua, New York, who said he planned to take up land near Coldwater.

Charles: "How do you go from Detroit?" Where is Coldwater?"

Sam: "We plan to go on the stage from Detroit over the Chicago road, which, I understand, passes near my kinfolk in Coldwater. Where are you going to locate?"

Charles: "In Oakland County. My father-in-law is there, two uncles, and two brothers-in-law are already there and have several desirable farms for us to consider."

Joshua Bangs and wife joined the group. They, too, were from New York, and were headed for Paw Paw in Southwestern Michigan, and would go over the Territorial road,—the Chicago turnpike—to Paw Paw. Mr. and Mrs. Jonathan B. Graham from Connecticut introduced themselves. They were to drive the oxen and wagon with household goods to Hillsdale. The Severances became acquainted with families who were to settle in Flint, Saginaw, Mt. Clemens, Pontiac, and other points in the state. While this small group was having a jolly time,

MICHIGAN TRAILMAKERS

some one suggested that they all sing the Emigrant Song which was familiar to most emigrants as it had been sung in their homes in the east. Charles and Ezra, Martha and Susan, were good singers. The quartet started it and everybody sang. Four stanzas follow:

> "My eastern friends who wish to find
> A country that will suit your mind,
> Where comforts all are near at hand,
> Had better come to Michigan.
>
> Here is the place to live at ease,
> To work or play, just as you please;
> With little prudence any man
> Can soon get rich in Michigan.
>
> We here have soils of various kinds
> To suit men who have different minds,
> Prairies, openings, timbered land,
> And burr oak plains, in Michigan.
>
> You who would wish to hunt and fish
> Can find all kinds of game you wish;
> Our deer and turkey, they are grand,
> Our fish is good in Michigan."

Also, Michigan's popular New England song:

"Come, all ye Yankee farmers who wish to change your lot,
Who've spunk enough to trail beyond your native spot,
And leave behind the village where Pa and Ma do stay,
Come follow me, and settle in Michigania,—
Yea, Yea, yea, in Michigania,—Detroit."

After this song, they sang hymns such as Martin Luther's:

> "A mighty fortress is our God
> A bulwark never failing;
> Our helper he, amid the flood
> Of mortal ills prevailing
> For still our ancient foe
> Doth seek to work us woe
> His craft and power are great
> And armed with cruel hate,
> On earth is not his equal."

They were fond of hymns as they were devout people with strong religious convictions and felt their dependence upon God and looked to his protection from harm and for guidance.

In the late afternoon a strong wind blew up from the south and the lake showed signs of disturbances. The sky was overcast with rain and wind clouds. The ship began to roll and toss heavily. Martha was nervous and anxious and fearful as well as many other mothers on the ship. Charles and Ezra were stolidly built, muscular, courageous, full of life, and were not afraid of the turbulent sea. Lewis clung to his father's right leg and cried: "Take me daddy, me so sick in my tummy." His father took him and held him in his arms. Ezra helped the women and little Charles into the cabin. The lake became rougher, white caps appeared on the water in every direction. The steamboat was tossed about like a cork on the waves, now riding on the crest of a great billow, now down in the trough swinging to the right front and the left back so the passengers

MICHIGAN TRAILMAKERS

had to cling to the ship's stationary chairs, and the door jambs to keep them from sliding across the cabin and to keep those on the outside from slipping off the deck into the water. Strong men as well as weak tired women, children, and young people became sea-sick. When the storm ceased three hours later, the cabin floor and the deck were sickly, ill-smelling places.

The next day about noon, little Lewis rushed to his mother in the cabin and in great excitement pointed to the forest to the left and exclaimed: "Michie, Michie." The whole party went on the forward deck.

Martha: "Can that be Michigan?"

Charles: "That is a shore line. That island must be Bois Blank, which Caleb wrote about. Isn't it beautiful with its grove of hardwood trees and clean hard shore line?"

Ezra noticing trees on the shore to the right: "That must be Canada. See how the lake is narrowing up. We must be entering the Detroit River."

Susan: "What are those buildings on shore to the left and ahead of us?"

Ezra: "Fort Wayne. The U. S. government maintains a fort here to control the Detroit River. It was built for protection during the French and Indian wars. This is the fort that General Hull ignominiously surrendered in 1812."

Charles: "I have heard of those Indian wars and of Chief Tecumseh and Chief Pontiac in whose honor towns were named."

Martha, looking ahead: "What are those queer looking buildings on the bank ahead of us?"

Charles replied: "Oh! that's Detroit. Don't you recall that Caleb told us about those queer low French buildings."

The Michigan edged up to the wharf at the foot of Woodward Avenue, and was made fast by the great ropes, then the drawbridge was let down and the passengers began to file out. The Severances waited on deck, and reviewed the motley crowd assembling at the wharf to see the ship come in and to get jobs at unloading the freight or to secure roomers for the hotels.

Martha: "We must be in a foreign port. The houses and stores are queer. I have never seen such women before."

Ezra: "Caleb said that Detroit was originally a French town. Those men must be Frenchmen and Indians."

They hastened down and went ashore, each man carrying a boy and steadying a woman. Then the men looked to the oxen and covered wagon and baggage and freight in the hold of the ship. In the meantime, the women and children watched the deck hands unload the freight and were astonished at the quantity and quality of the shipment. There were barrels of flour, barrels of salt pork, barrels of sugar, bags of coffee, plows and parts of plows such as the colter, the steel points, and the shares, and chains and harness, ox yokes, oxen, cows for milk, pigs, chickens, horses, and every such thing that a growing city and towns and pioneer settlements might need. The covered wagon was soon ready to move with its precious freight. It moved up Woodward to Jefferson Avenue, then to Cousin Thomas Palmer's home at the corner of Fort and Shelby Streets.

Thomas Palmer, the father of Senator Thomas W. Palmer, was born at Ashford, Connecticut, February 4, 1789. When eighteen years of age, in company with an older brother, Friend, he became an itinerant merchant, a common vocation in New England at that time. They set out with a stock of general merchandise and a span of horses, traveling through western Canada until they reached Malden. Here they established themselves and carried on a successful business until the War of 1812, when they were made prisoners. After being held five weeks and being unwilling to take the oath of allegiance to Great Britain, they were transported over the river to Monguagon. They proceeded to Detroit and were very soon again made prisoners. This time they were released on parole and returned to Connecticut. Again they set out with merchandise and made their headquarters at Canandaigua, New York. Thomas departed through Canada to Detroit, arriving on June 16, 1815. He formed a partnership with his brother, Friend, to sell general merchandise with eastern headquarters at Canandaigua, New York. Thomas was the western representative of the firm. They had a prosperous business and soon shared the partnership with their brother, John, under the firm of F. J. T. Palmer. A few years later, Thomas became a contractor and built the territorial capitol in Detroit on the site of the present high school building and received in payment ten thousand acres of land adjacent to the town. He owned the village of Palmer which later was called St. Clair. He was considered a wealthy man in 1835, when his cousins and their husbands visited him on their way to settle in the woods of Oakland County. His little boy, Thomas W., who in later years became a national figure was of the same age, four years, as Martha's Lewis, but the children did not get acquainted in so short a time as a day and a night. Thomas urged Charles and Ezra to go next day to the Land Office in Detroit and find the location of acreages not yet sold and added: "The tide of immigration has set in. Hundreds of home seekers and land speculators are being landed from the steamers every day and hundreds more are coming over land through Ohio into southern and western Michigan." Detroit, itself, in the words of Hamlin Garland: "Was at first a sadly disappointing small and shabby village but a closer study developed the flavor of its frontier character. Red men, trappers, lumbermen, fishermen, fur merchants and soldiers mingled on easy terms in its muddy streets, while confident pigs and grazing cows gave evidence of comfort as well as of a good natural rural tolerance of nuisances on the part of its citizens."

CHAPTER III

FIRST WINTER IN MICHIGAN 1835-36

There were three main highways leading out of Detroit to the various points in Michigan. The Chicago turnpike was a territorial road starting at Detroit, passing through the "dismal swamp" before reaching Dearborn and passing on through Ypsilanti, Saline, Hillsdale, Coldwater, and ending in Chicago. A stage line had been established over this route and stage coaches were making regular trips in 1835. Harriet Martineau described a stage coach ride in her *Society of America*. Immigrants planning to settle in southern Michigan would invariably take either the stage coach or drive their oxen and covered wagons along this turnpike across the River Rouge and get stuck in the mud and water of the "dismal swamp." The River Rouge which carried the water off in time had so slight a gradient that one could not tell in which direction the water was running without throwing a chip or a stick into the stream to see in which direction it floated.

The Detroit and Pontiac road directed the immigrants toward Flint and Saginaw, also to Mount Clemens. They would cross the Clinton River at Pontiac, then penetrate the wilderness to the west, north and east. This highway had been improved for five or six miles out of Detroit by a corduroy construction of logs laid close together side by side across the wagon track and covered with dirt. The mud beyond the corduroy was so deep and sticky that a team of oxen could scarcely manage an empty wagon. Mr. Palmer told his guests the following story which although absurd, frightened the women and lessened the courage of the men. He said: "Several strangers looking for land started out on this Pontiac road and were winding their way over bogs and around stumps, sometimes on this side of the road, sometimes on that, and in constant danger of being swallowed up in the mire. One of these men, a little in advance of the rest of them discovered as he thought a good beaver hat, lying on the center of the road. He called to his companions to halt while he ventured to secure it at the risk of his life. He waded out, more than knee deep to the spot, and seizing the hat to his surprise he found a live man's head under it, but on lustily raising a cry for help, the stranger in the mire declined all assistance saying, "Just leave me alone, I have a good horse under me, and have just found bottom, go on, gentlemen, and mind your own business."

The third highway was the Grand River road passing through swamps, over rivers, through Redford to Farmington and to Novi,—a wagon road part of the way, a mere trail the remainder of the way. In later years, this was known as the Grand River turnpike from Detroit to Lansing, the capital of the state. This highway led the immigrants into the very heart of the state. Like the other roads radiating from Detroit, it was corduroy for several miles. The party got an early start, made good time about three miles an hour until they left the improved road. Then trouble began. The nigh ox mired in the mud and went down. The wagon stuck; the water was a foot deep caused by recent rain. Martha and Susan got out of the wagon, stepped into the water and with fearful hearts, made their way to higher ground with the help of the men. Then the children were carried forward, followed by the crate of hens, and pigs, and baggage until the wagon was empty. The oxen renewed their courage and their strength and brought forward the empty wagon. Caleb had a similar experience. His one horse and light wagon stuck here when he moved to Farmington a few years earlier. The horse did well to make the slough and draw a light wagon through it. The Surveyor had not exaggerated the condition of the terrible morasses around Detroit. It was late at night when the oxen pulled up to the door of Caleb's log house where the light from the tallow dips welcomed them. They all were muddy and wet and tired; the children were cross. Words cannot express their gratitude and happiness with the warmth of the house and the joyous welcome of the Lambs. It was a glad reunion and homecoming after several years' separation. Charles, Martha, Ezra, and Susan recounted the hardships of the journey and the pleasures of the trip and conveyed greetings from the friends and kinfolk of New Hampshire and of Geneva. They visited till late at night, then followed a reading of a selection from the Bible and the evening prayer by Caleb and the singing of,

> "Guide me, O thou great Jehovah,
>   Pilgrim through this barren land;
> I am weak, but thou art mighty,
>   Hold me by thy powerful hand;
> Bread of Heaven,
>   Feed me till I want no more."

And
> "O God! our help in ages past,
>   Our hope for years to come,
> Our shelter from the stormy blast,
>   And our eternal home."

The early settlers, particularly those from New England, felt their dependence upon their heavenly Father. It was He who kept them from harm when the storms raged over Lake Erie and buoyed them up on their sea of troubles. The Hartsoughs had arrived in their "schooner" a month earlier and settled at Redford. The Severances and Hartsoughs were heartily welcomed into the homes of the members of the Baptist Church of which Caleb Lamb and his father, Nehemiah, have been pastors. It was like a great homecoming. The ties of kinfolk, especially in a new settlement in the woods, are vibrant and strong. They all desired to settle in Farmington but acreage in this vicinity had all been "proved."

Caleb told them: "There are few government holdings in this vicinity still available. Immigration is reaching its flood tide. Thousands enter Detroit daily from the steamers and many more are coming in as Uncle Wells did, over the trails around the southern shore of lake Erie, and over the roads through Canada and across the river at Detroit. There are hundreds of land speculators arriving every day. Beware of them. I know the location of acreages in the townships of Farmington, Commerce, Novi, and other lands near Northville and Plymouth."

The next morning Caleb, Charles, Wells, and Ezra started northwest on a tramp to visit new settlers and to locate farms. They followed the trail running due west which later divided the township of Farmington from West Bloomfield, and stopped before a log house on top of a large hill. Theron Murray called to them. Caleb replied: "I am Caleb Lamb from Farmington. These men are Charles and Ezra Severance and Wells Hartsough from New York. We want to locate three one hundred-sixty-acre farms. Can you tell us where there are some good acreages?" Theron: "Why yes, I settled on this hill three years ago and have a good farm. The farms west on this road are taken but I think there is a quarter section over north on the Commerce road." Caleb: "Anything around Walled Lake or Novi?" Theron: "I don't know." A mile farther on they came upon another clearing with a good house and a field of corn which the farmer was cutting. Caleb called: "Hello, there." "Hello" came back with a joyous ring. "Who are you?" The men were introduced in pioneer fashion. Emmett Green said he came from Rhode Island in 1832, had located this half section of timberland with rich clay soil. "I am entirely satisfied" he said. "This will be a great farm in a few years. Michigan will be a great state." He indicated the land north on the Commerce road and one on the Walled Lake road. The men were pleased with the corn crop and the appearance of the soil under cultivation. They explored the farm indicated. "This is a quarter section of oak openings. It wouldn't be difficult to get an early crop," said Charles. "I don't care for the large tamarack marsh," said Ezra. Caleb observed that a house could be erected on the rise of ground near the creek and that it could be easily constructed of those fine, tall tamarack trees. Wells said there was upland enough for any family. "Look at those fine oaks, maples and hickories."

They next stopped at John Welfare's on the way to the lake. He had a family of four boys. After a short visit, the trampers moved on, ascended the next hill and looked beyond. "By golly" exclaimed Charles, "if there ain't water." They hurried down the hill and stood on the shore of a beautiful lake. "It is larger and pettier than our lake in Washington, New Hampshire." "About a mile across and five miles around is my guess," said Caleb. The October sun was shining warm and bright with an occasional fleecy cloud floating below it. As the men looked upon the water, the color changed as the clouds cast fleeting shadows on the water. It was a light green then a dark geen and then a dark blue. The trees were mirrored on the glassy surface of the water. "What a restful scene," observed Uncle Wells. "Do you see the canoes on the lake manned by Indians?" asked Caleb. "Are they wild and dangerous and are they around this lake all the year?" asked Charles. Caleb: "They are friendly, neighborly and will do the whites no harm while they are sober. There is a trading post about a half mile to the west of us kept by Prentice and King where the Indians may trade furs, venison and fish for trinkets, pork, flour, potatoes, and the like. The Indians have a garden farther around where they raise potatoes, beans and squash, and they have set out an orchard. I preached at the village two years ago. Only a few of the Indians stay the year round. They go into winter quarters near Niles, way west of here." "How far is it to my farm from here?" asked Charles. Having spent his boyhood on a lakeshore, this beautiful sheet of water was making a strong appeal to him. "Two and a half miles," replied Caleb. "Let's move on or we won't reach Uncle Horace Johns's place tonight. Uncle Horace also had migrated from New York, bringing all his effects from Genessee County ten years before,—1825,—and was already a prosperous farmer with a good acreage and good buildings not far west of Novi. They arrived at a clearing as the sun was sinking into the great forest in the west. They saw a large portly man with a milk pail on his arm walking erect with two small boys at his heels. Caleb called to him, "Hello! Uncle Horace!" He turned facing the men, then exclaimed: "Well!! Well!! Brother Wells; and Caleb, how are you and these nephews I haven't seen before? Come on in the house. Content will want to see you. Caleb told me last summer that you all were coming. When did you arrive? (Turning to Wells) How are Thankful and the children?" Content came in and was overjoyed to see her kinfolk. Life in the woods where the housewife can see no one for weeks at a time becomes unendurable. Long days with hard work and with no one but the children and husband to talk with become dreary. Ezra told of his home in Washington, New Hampshire and his trip to Geneva, New York, Charles described his trip over the Erie Canal and of the schooner from Geneva to Buffalo and the boat trip across Lake Erie. Wells told how he travelled to Buffalo and Detroit bringing all his belongings in a covered wagon from Gorham, New York and how they managed to cross the "dismal swamp" on the state road running from Detroit through Farmington. "Now," he said, "we all are here in this country of beautiful lakes and rivers and forests to make homes for ourselves." It was long after midnight when Uncle Horace drew in the latch string and put on the night log and banked the fire.

They were up with the sun and out to see the fine draft horses, the good cows and calves and hogs and chickens, also the new frame barn and the orchard back of it which had been stripped of its baldwins, northern spies, and greenings. Off to the right was a forty-acre field of winter wheat covering the ground with its deep green blades. To the left, was the corn already cut and shocked,—which was pleasing to the eyes of these new farmers. Uncle Horace pointed out a tract of a

MICHIGAN TRAILMAKERS 29

hundred and sixty acres near Northville which he said lies well for drainage. The soil is heavy and rich like the soil of this farm.

The land office in Detroit was a busy place. Every day hundreds of immigrants disembarked from the ships at the foot of Woodward Avenue and other hundreds came overland through northern Ohio to find homes in Michigan. Land agents were never so busy. They had explored the lands throughout southern Michigan and knew where the best farming and timberlands were to be found. They had purchased large tracts to sell again at a higher price than $1.25 an acre which had to be paid to the United States Government.

When Charles, Ezra, and Wells the next day went to the land office in Detroit to buy their farms, they were accosted several times by agents of the several land companies who had land for sale anywhere in southern Michigan and wanted to show their good farms. The agents frequented the hotels in Detroit and in the villages where immigrants were sure to come. There was a mania for land speculation. A speculator coming into the state, of whatever calling or profession, explored the country, then went straight to one of the land offices and took up as many acres in a desired location as his means would permit and immediately put a price upon the land from two times to thirty or forty times the original cost. If he were fortunate to secure a tract on one of the territorial roads, especially the Chicago road or the Detroit and Grand River road, or near the crossing of a river or adjacent to a possible water power, he at once called a surveyor and plotted a town with elegant streets, broad public squares, reservations for churches, courthouses, schools, and colleges. Charles had decided on the half section near Walled Lake. Ezra bought the farm near Northville and Wells settled at the "Sand hill" later called Redford but within a few years he purchased a tract near Ezra's which had rich soil and raised bumper crops.

They remained with the Lambs in Farmington until Ezra's house, near Northville, about five miles away was ready for occupancy. The men soon cleared a half acre and made the logs ready for the house. With the help of Uncle Wells and the neighbors, living within a radius of five or six miles, the boys raised the log house and roofed it within a month. Then followed a clearing and the erection of a barn for the oxen, chickens and pigs. Early in November (1835) the two families were settled in the new house for the winter which was a severely cold winter with an unusually heavy snow fall. The settlers were literally "snow bound" for several weeks, the snow remaining on the ground well into March. In the new home, Martha enjoyed more quiet and rest than she had experienced since she left Geneva. This quiet moderate life was good for her nerves. She stood the journey from New York with its various hardships remarkably well for one who was not vigorous, nor sturdy and who had the responsibility and care of two sturdy little boys. Her third boy was presented to the family December 15 and given the name, Thomas Chalkley. Susan was younger and vivacious, with fewer responsibilities and fewer occasions for worry. Her work was strenuous, as the responsibility of the home fell upon her shoulders during Martha's illness and she was looking forward fearfully and courageously toward motherhood in the spring.

The woodman's ax could have been heard in the clearing back of the barn from early morning until late at night. The men cleared off a lot for the early planting of potatoes in the spring. They were strong and hardy, and stout and full of energy. The days were too short for the work they wanted to do. They became expert with their axes.

CHAPTER IV

THE NEW HOME IN COMMERCE TOWNSHIP

The brothers worked early and late during the winter and early spring of 1836 in clearing up four or five acres so that Ezra might plant some early potatoes and corn, as corn meal, potatoes, pork or wild game were their principal food. Sufficient must be raised to carry the family through the next winter as wheat could not be sowed until August or September to be reaped the following spring. They then gave attention to Charles' farm twelve miles away. It was necessary to provide a house for shelter and a clearing where he too might raise sufficient food for his growing family. Charles' hundred and eighty acres lay part in West Bloomfield and part in Commerce township. The north and south trail on the town line therefore, intersected his farm which extended west into Commerce about a mile. The north side of that portion of the farm in Commerce township embraced a large acreage of marsh, part of which was covered with grass, the rest was thickly studded with tall cedar and tamarack trees. The trees grew straight up thirty, forty, or fifty feet, straight as a mast, with small trunks six inches to eight inches in thickness with small branches at the tops. There was so much rosin in the wood that it burned green like dry pine and made a hot fire. The south side of the farm and the east end located in West Bloomfield was heavily timbered with hard wood trees,—red and white oak, hard and soft maple, shagbark hickory, walnut, butternut, and the soft woods, such as the basswood, willows and the chestnut. The farm had a variety of soil from the heavy clay on the east to the light clay and sandy soil on the west, with muck on the north spreading out to the timbered marsh. They chose a site for the house and barn,—a rise of ground facing the trail on the east, about the center of the farm north and south, an oak opening on light soil; consequently, well drained with a creek near by and a spring not far away. The timber was light with considerable underbrush. The clearing was made. Logs twenty-two feet long for the sides of the house and eighteen feet long for the ends were cut in the marsh and drawn to the site of the house. Trunks of red oak trees were cut into six feet logs and split into thin flat pieces for the roof and called "shakes". A lot of wooden pegs of different sizes were made by splitting six inch lengths of red oak logs into pegs.

Then came the house raising party. Charles visited the neighbors on the north and east. Ezra visited those south and southeast and invited them to assist in raising the house. "I'll be there" was the cheerful response.

The neighbors came early on "raising day." They were never too busy to lend a hand on such occasions. Eldad Smith, Seymour Devereaux, and Ezekiel Dye came from the north; Harvey Dodge and

John Coe came from the east; Theron Murray, Solomon Stilson, and Addis Emmet Greene from the southeast on the Farmington trail. Mr. Greene was chosen boss because he knew how and had bossed previous jobs. The corner men were Dye and Devereaux; Coe and Stilson, who trimmed the ends of the logs and made good joints. The others rolled the logs and lifted them into place which was easy for the first half dozen courses. Skids were provided for the courses higher up. When the log was pushed up as high as the men could reach, they took pikes made of crotched poles and rolled the logs into place. They finished before sunset. Martha and Susan furnished hot coffee, hot bread and meat. It was the custom for the owner to furnish a jug of whisky for such an occasion, but Charles's neighbors did not quit the job because the whisky was lacking. There was a wave of a national temperance movement sweeping over Michigan at this time. The W. C. T. U. was campaigning in the interests of the white ribbon movement. Men, women and children were being asked to "sign the pledge." Many of the early settlers were teetotallers. The men worked hard at "logging bees" and "house raisings" and enjoyed the chaff and banter and stories and jokes and songs. Charles and Ezra put on the ridge and rafters, next day and the "shakes" which covered the roof. There were three rows of shakes, six feet long overlapping ends and fastened down with a long sapling laid lengthwise of the building across each layer of "shakes". The ends of the saplings were made fast by pegs or withes. The cracks between the logs were filled in with split pieces of wood called clinkers and fastened in with clay which had been wet and worked until it became stiff mud. The split basswood logs laid crosswise of the room and fastened down with wooden pegs constituted the floor which was smoothed by use of the adz. The attic floor was also made of basswood.

The house was twenty-two feet long by eighteen feet wide with the side paralled with the road or trail. There was a door and a window in either side, that is, one in the front and one in the rear of the house. The door had wooden hinges, a wooden latch on the inside which was raised from the outside by a latch string or strap which was pushed out through the hole and hung down on the outside. To lock the house, they pulled the latch string inside. The window panes were fastened in with wooden pegs.

The fireplace was the center of family life. The fire cooked the food, warmed the room, and furnished light in the evening. It was a great comfort and a great pleasure to sit by the open fireplace and watch the logs burn and to toast the apples and to roast the spare ribs by the open fire. The early settlers had "wood to burn", so they constructed their fireplace large enough to take in great logs which had to be rolled over the floor with a cant hook. Charles built a fireplace six feet wide by four feet deep with a chimney that was two by four feet at the top. Into the log back of the fireplace, he drove two iron eyes on which to hang a crane which extended about a foot into the room. The floor and back of the fireplace were made of clear clay a foot thick at the bottom but thinner when it reached the sticks on the back. The chimney was built of sticks and clay in much the same way that brick and mortar are used today. The sticks were cut the right length for the sides and back and front of the chimney, laid up in clay, and plastered on the inside with clay, so the sticks would not catch fire. Before a fire was started, a back log five feet long and possibly twenty inches thick was rolled into the back of the fireplace. Then two green sticks, six or eight inches in diameter and three feet long, with ends against the back log were the andirons. Then a fore stick was laid on the front ends of the andirons, and a fire was laid between the back log and the fore stick, which furnished cheer and comfort and light and heat for at least twenty-four hours.

During the next few busy days, the men made a barn for the oxen and a stockade enclosure so the bears and wolves could not reach them. They made also some tables and chairs and bedsteads. The bedsteads were made by boring holes into the floor and driving crotched sticks into the holes, then by laying poles in the crotches and sticks across the poles and covering the whole with elm bark. Blankets and feather ticks softened to some extent the rough spots.

At the end of the week, the oxen and wagon came over from Northville bringing Martha, the new baby, Thomas, Charles L. and Lewis and the household goods,—the bedding, cooking utensils, the spinning wheel, the small loom—the chickens, and the hogs. Then Martha settled in her new home. In the north end was the fireplace, and on the mantel above was the old clock. Charles set the crane with various sized pot hooks in the fireplace. The bake kettle and pots and tin pans, tea kettle, frying pans had a place to the right of the fireplace. The bake kettle was a flat low kettle with a cast iron cover, the top of which turned up an inch or two to hold the coals. To bake bread, cover with the hot iron cover, set the kettle on the hot coals, and put a shovelful of coals on top the lid and let it cook. To the left of the fireplace were shelves against the walls for dishes and for potatoes, meat, flour, milk pans, tin cups, dippers, and the pail of water for cooking. Near the center of the room was the dining room table and in the south end of the room were the beds on one side, the spinning wheel and the loom for weaving the cloth on the other. In the southeast corner, was the ladder by which the children could climb to the beds in the attic which were spread on the floor. Other conveniences were added as the needs arose. Outside the house beside the back door stood a wash stand with a pail of water on it brought from the creek about forty rods north of the house, and a towel hanging to a wooden peg driven into a log three feet from the ground.

In the early morning the crows discovered the new house. They sailed over and around and glided up and down and looked the house and barns over and cawed and cawed notifying their kindred far and near that here was another settlement and that there might be more corn to dig up. The hawks sailed high but kept sharp eyes on the clearing in search of young chickens. A saucy little chipmunk climbed to the top of a paling of the stockade and fretted and scolded. A big gray squirrel got a vantage place in the branches of a nearby oak and made a terrible fuss. The robins were more sociable, ran along the ground, came near the back door and greeted Charles as he came. He called to Martha and the children to step outside and see the wild life all about them which was giving them a morning welcome. After dark they could hear bruin who came under darkness to make his visit and his exploration, but he didn't find any choice little pigs nor did Mr. Fox find any hens. The hoot of the owl and the song of the whip-poor-will and the baying of Eldad Smith's hound broke the stillness of the night.

The snow had gone. Spring was near at hand. Charles was up before the sun, had milked the cow, fed the oxen, and felled several trees before breakfast. He cleared a few acres south of the house first so that the midday sun could shine on the roof. Martha told him they must have sun to keep the house floors dry and to warm the south side where the children might play. He piled the brush to the east and to the west of the clearing and felled the trees toward the brush so that by use of a cant hook and the oxen he could roll the logs into the brush and make a temporary fence. He plowed among trees in the oak opening south of the house but it was impossible to plow among the stumps in the thicker timber until the fire had burned over the clearing. He chopped into the soil and roots of these hardwood stumps with his ax so that he could plant some early corn. The soil he plowed was leveled up with the crotched log iron-toothed drag which was drawn back and forth over the plowed surface and weighted down with a large stone or stump tied to the top. He planted part to potatoes, part he sowed to oats and later plowing he planted to corn when the red oak buds got to be the size of a squirrel's ear.

Martha had carefully tucked away some beet seed and peas and beans when she left New York. She surprised Charles by bringing them out for planting. She had not forgotten the morning glory, nasturtium, sweet william which she planted later in her flower garden near the house. The morning glories were trained to climb up around the back door and window and up the south end to cover the logs and add beauty and charm to the setting of this log house hidden away in the forest.

CHAPTER V
LIFE IN THE WOODS

I

Easter Sunday was a balmy day, a gentle breeze came in from the west after a warm April shower. The fleecy clouds were hurrying away to the east; the blue dome of the sky could be seen above them. The wild birds were singing their happy songs in the woods. The frogs in the marsh were croaking their loudest. The tree toads, which made so much noise before the shower, were quiet. A beautiful Easter day made glad the hearts of the pioneers and the wild birds and the wild animals. Martha, the children, and Charles felt the effects of the day. Martha said: "Let's go to church today."

Martha was the daughter of a minister, was devoted to the church and found her greatest pleasure in church work. She felt the presence of God in her every day life, was grateful to Him for His guidance and care on their trip to this new country and in the selection of the present farm home. She was grateful for her boys and felt the responsibility for training them in right living and in the development and care of their bodies. She found great comfort and consolation in prayer. The boys said their prayers to her every night before they ascended the ladder to the attic.

MICHIGAN TRAILMAKERS 41

Since settling so far from church, she had been denied the privilege of church attendance on account of those sticky clay roads leading to the church at West Farmington and on account of bad weather in early spring. Tom was only a few months old. She was afraid to take him so far away in bad weather. She had longed for the opportunity to go to church again. Here was the day, this Easter Day, when Charles yoked the oxen and went to church with his family. Charles, too, wanted to go. The work of chopping and clearing was new to him. He couldn't stand seven days a week of it. Both of them were hungry for some one to talk with. Shut up on the little clearing where neighbors were far away and no one but themselves and the children to talk with, living became monotonous, they became restless and uneasy. They started to church this Easter Day with cares and responsibilities weighing heavily upon them; they returned at the close of the day with a freshness and a happiness which they had not experienced for weeks.

Elder Lamb (Caleb) was a pioneer missionary preacher who had experienced all the hardships that many of them had suffered and had enjoyed as many blessings as any of his church members. He preached with a sympathetic heart. Caleb was a favorite brother of Martha in whose preaching and personality and home life she took great delight. Church meeting on this Easter was like a reunion. Martha and Susan and Aunt Thankful had so much to talk about, so much had happened since they had landed at Caleb's last October. Tom had come into Martha's home, Horace into Susan's, and Sarah into Aunt Thankful's home. The coming of children into the homes of pioneers when doctors were few and far away caused much suffering and great anxiety, but here were a healthy lot of babies and youngsters. The outdoor life was conducive to health.

Wells Hartsough was already dissatisfied with his Sand Hill farm. He could work the soil as soon as a rain was over, but discovered it had no depth and he probably could not produce good crops. He sold it largely on account of its location, near Detroit, and took up acreage from the government near Plymouth.

Ezra was as far along as Charles with his spring sowing and planting. Prospects were good for crops. Potatoes and corn were necessities for the family sustenance and for the livestock the next fall and winter.

Martha (on the way home): "Did Caleb tell his new plans about Hahnemann?"

Charles: "No. Is he a new comer, too? Is he to settle in our neighborhood? Sounds like a German name."

Martha: "Oh, no, Charles, he was a German doctor and was never in America. He instituted a new system of medicine which is producing wonderful results. His slogan is 'Like cures like'."

Charles: "What does that mean?"

Martha: "Caleb said the theory is that if the poison, Belladonna would produce a headache, it

MICHIGAN TRAILMAKERS 43

would cure a headache when started. Aconite would produce fever when taken in moderate doses, consequently, when a child has fever, give him aconite to stop it. Seems a very simple medical principle."

Charles: "What has Caleb to do with it?"

Martha: "He plans to give up preaching, move to Detroit, and study this system of medicine which he said is called by some the 'Hahnemann System', by others the 'Homoeopathic System of Medicine.' Instead of large doses of nasty medicine given by the regular or allopathic physicians the homoeopathic doctor gives sugar coated pills, small doses in liquid form and in powdered form."

Charles: "It will be fine to have a doctor in the family."

II

When Martha got the children ready for bed and heard their prayers, Lewis, with eyes wide open, spoke up: "Ma, I want to see the injuns." 'Lonzo said, "Their fierce, painted faces, feathers on the caps and great bos' an' arrows in their hands are great. Lot of 'em at the Lake. Ma, why don't we go to church at the Lake so we can see the injuns?"

Martha: "Skip up to bed, take Charles with you, I will talk to your pa about it."

The next morning Lewis came down the ladder early. As soon as his father came into breakfast, he began jumping up and down and begging. "Pa, I want to see the injuns." Little Charles L. piped up: "Me want to see injuns, Pa."

Martha: "Daddy we better take a day off to see the Indians at Walled Lake village. John Welfare told me that most of them have gone west on account of a Treaty with the government. This may be their last summer."

In August, when the corn was laid by, Charles yoked the oxen to the wagon, took the family and the Welfares and went to town. They stopped within a few rods of the Indians' summer camp, the little settlement of tepees. "Who is the big Indian sitting in front of the tent? He has feathers in his cap, rings in his ears, mocassins on his feet, reddish paint on his face, smoking a pipe," asked George. "I bet that's the chief," said Lewis. "See the ponies off to the right. My, I would like to ride one," said John. "O shucks! they're too wild for you, they would throw you in a jiffy," replied Lewis. Martha noticed the garden with sweet corn in the ear and the apple orchard beyond. John who had something of a drawl in his speech, always spoke slowly and you would think he was weighing every word, told the story of Prentice and King who kept the trading post where the Indians exchanged their furs, berries, venison, deer skins, and the like, for pork, flour and trinkets. They were young men from Maine and in a sense fugitives from justice. Prentice fell in love with one of Maine's fair maidens, so did a rival. Jealousy and rivalry in love is a very serious matter. Prentice was devoted to Susan. His rival was equally devoted to Susan. Susan could not dismiss either. The truth is she loved them both but only one could have her, and which one, that was to be settled by a duel. They met early Saturday in a field a mile out of town. King was Prentice's second. When the smoke cleared away, Prentice's rival was dead and he, himself, was severely wounded. He and King had to leave the state. Prentice being jilted by the girl he loved became disgusted and started for the west with King. Here they were in a trading post at Walled Lake.

They were not unconscious of the beauties of the Indian maidens. The squaw of Chief Sheskone often came to the store with her daughters, Wild Flower and Dawn, who were of marriageable age. Dawn was rightly named. She stood erect, head up, her black hair pushed straight back and fastened to a chip on the back of her head. The red paint on her cheeks gave her a ruddy appearance which harmonized with her black hair. Her black eyes sparkled with life, they were bewitching. Add to this the silver earrings and the necklace, the mocassins, trimmed with porcupine quills, the buckskin leggings, with fuzzy frills at the bottom and fastened with a garter below the knee, the broadcloth skirt suspended from the hips and extending below the knees and over her shoulders her own red blanket. Wild Flower was equally attractive. Their charm was not so much in their dress as in their carriage, light and fleet of foot, alert, wary, independent. Besides, these Indians were nearly civilized. They were human, they fished and hunted with the Americans. The love flames which were extinguished in the hearts of Prentice and King broke out again.

They consulted Chief Sheskone, and, not knowing this tribe, offered to buy Dawn and Wild Flower for their wives. No, not for sale. A week or two later, Dawn and Wild Flower entered the trading post carrying food for Prentice and King, the Indian method of announcing their engagement. Then followed, in accordance with Indian custom, the presents to the would be mother-in-law and then the gifts of the Chief and his Squaw to Prentice and King, their sons-in-law.

According to treaty agreements, this tribe,—the Pottawottomies vacated their hunting ground in Michigan in 1833 and took up land west of the Mississippi. Prentice and King became a part of the tribe and went with it.

They were transferred first to Northwest Missouri, opposite Fort Leavenworth, then to Iowa near Council Bluffs and thirty years later to Indian territory.

On the road home, after they left the Welfares at their home, they saw approaching them, a tall man on horseback. He had a tall crowned hat which emphasized the height of the rider who was trying to read as his tired bay mare slowly made her way. When he came alongside, his horse and the oxen stopped. "Hello, stranger," said he, "You must be new in these parts." "We are," replied Charles, "We live in the first house, north on the Commerce road. My name is Charles Severance. Do you live hereabout?" Stranger: "Yes, at the Lake. My name is Tenny. I carry the mail from Farmington to the Lake, the Overland Mail. I haven't much mail today, (bending forward and removing the big hat dropping the crown down first so that the letters would not fall out). I used to carry the mail in my pockets but our town is getting larger, consequently, more letters are received and a newspaper or two. Here is a copy of the Detroit Free Press for Jesse Tuttle."

Charles: "The Welfare family and we have been to the Lake so the children could see the Indians. John told us the story of Prentice and King marrying Dawn and Wild Flower."

Tenny: "Mighty fine Indians. They are what is left of the Pottawottomie tribe which at one time occupied northern, eastern, and southern Michigan. They belong to the Algonquin tribe and are kin to the Ottawas whose famous chief was Pontiac who is said to have had a summer camp on a beautiful island in Orchard Lake about six miles from here. The Pottawottomies joined Pontiac in his war against the English and were defeated. Topanibee, a chief of the Pottawottomies for forty years, joined Tecumseh, the Shawnee chief when he waged war against General Harrison and was defeated at Tippecano. After every defeat the United States exacts more land from them until finally they will all disappear from this beautiful country which they have enjoyed so many years. Whisky is their worst enemy. I am a deacon in the Baptist Church, organized only three years ago. Be glad to see you at church. Good-by."

III

The "Logging bee" came in July. Charles had cleared about five acres for the wheat crop. Eldad Smith and Solomon Stilson came with their ox teams and chains and cant hooks and helped remove the logs and brush and put them into cords and piles to be burned when the brush and logs should dry out. Then the three ox teams were hitched to the great bull-plow which would cut off roots three or four inches thick and overturn small stumps without stopping the oxen and without breaking the plow. The plow had a sharp edged steel colter and a share of iron or steel and mould board of wood. Then came the dragging with the heavy spiked crotched harrow and the chopping off and pulling out of roots which had been broken by the plow, and the rooting out of stumps which had been overturned. Lewis tugged away on the smaller roots and carried them to piles for burning and helped to pile the brush when trees were felled, but the job for Lewis and Charles L. was to watch the cow and keep her close to the house.

About the first of September, Charles harrowed the wheat ground again and sowed his wheat. He tied the corner of the end of the grain bag to the edge of the mouth of the sack, put it over his head so the bag swung under his left arm. With his right hand he reached into the bag and drew out a handful of the precious yellow seed and began throwing it evenly over the ground as he walked across the plowed field on the east side, then he took three paces to the west, made a mark so he would know where to start back, then three paces farther west. Here he pushed a pole into the ground indicating the goal for his return. Then returning to his mark, he raised his head and walked straight to the goal pole at the other end of the field, scattering the golden grain evenly over the surface. After harrowing, the field was finished for the winter.

In the fall, he cut the buckwheat and set it up in bundles to dry. When the ground was frozen, he cleared a small area near the barn, making it as smooth as he could. This was the threshing floor for his buckwheat. After flailing it he took off the straw for bedding the oxen and swept up the kernels and tossed them into the air. The wind blew the chaff away, and the kernels fell to the ground, and were taken up and put into bags, taken to the grist mill in Farmington, and returned as buckwheat flour which, with potatoes, dried corn, beans, peas, corn meal and venison, wild turkey, squirrel and rabbit furnished the diet for the long winter months.

In July of 1837 came the wheat harvest. The cradle cut and laid the wheat in an even swath which was caught up and bound into bundles and shocked so the grain might dry and ripen. The threshing of wheat was a bigger job than threshing a few bushels of buckwheat. A board floor was made from logs which Charles had taken to the sawmill to be sawed into boards. This floor was surrounded by a temporary fence. Bundles of wheat were thrown in after the bands were cut, then the oxen driven into the enclosure were kept moving by frequent prodding with a stick in the hands of Lewis. After the wheat was treaded out or threshed, the straw was thrown out and the grain winnowed from the chaff by tossing shovels full of it into the air. The wind blew the chaff away, the grains of wheat fell to the floor. Some of the neighbors threshed wheat with the flail, others turned horses in to tread it out. Later the treadmill operated by one or two horses furnished the power for a thresher which beat out the grains of wheat but did not winnow it. This was introduced by S. Harger of West Bloomfield.

Martha was as busy in the house as Charles was outside. She had Lewis, Charles L. and baby Tom to keep clean, to be fed and clothed. She hadn't a great variety of food to serve. Potatoes, meat, Johnny cake and wheat bread were the staples and were served three times a day. In addition, there were huckleberries, strawberries, and blackberries in season picked by Martha and the boys. The old standby—pork—was frequently displaced by rabbit, squirrel, wild turkey and venison when Charles took time to go into the woods and get them. A typical dinner when the larder contained pork, potatoes and flour was: A large platter heaped up with steaming hot potatoes, and boiled pork, wheat bread, and a bowl of hot flour gravy made of flour and water seasoned with salt cooked up occasionally with a little grease gravy from a piece of meat. Crust coffee, made of wheat or rye, browned and steeped like coffee, was the hot drink used mostly for breakfast.

Tea, coffee and sugar were luxuries not afforded during the first years in the woods. Sweetening was made from wild honey and maple syrup, made in early spring by boiling down sap from the sugar maple trees. Mush and milk was the supper dish for the children.

The family sat down to supper after the day's work was done, usually after sundown. The room was lighted by the blaze of burning hickory bark and tamarack sticks so that one sitting near the fireplace could read a newspaper. The table had the additional light of tallow candles when there was sufficient tallow. At other times a twisted rag with one end coiled in a saucer of lard or tallow and the other end lighted was the evening taper. Many a night after the dishes were washed and the family in bed, Martha ran the spinning wheel and the handloom making cloth for the shirts, coats and pantaloons for the boys and for Charles.

"Early to bed and early to rise
Makes a man healthy and wise"

was observed by the men and children but not by the wives. "Late to bed and early to rise" expressed the habits of Martha and many other mothers. The habit was not conducive to health. Martha was not robust, she was delicate. She worked hard and late so that she might keep her family clothed and fed.

IV

While the Hartsoughs and Severances were clearing their farms and making their homes liveable, thousands of speculators and pioneers were rushing into Michigan and other western states and buying up all the good land they could get. The sales of western lands in 1831 brought the United States Government $2,300,000 while in 1837 the amount was $24,900,000. In Michigan, the total sales up to 1835 was 2,030,341 acres while in the year 1836, 4,031,114 acres were sold and paid for in paper money. When the Government required specie in payment for Federal lands in 1837, fewer acres were purchased. The situation in Michigan was aggravated by the "Free Bank Act" of January 1837 which required no special charter for the establishment of banks. Any persons desirous of forming an association for the banking business might do so by subscribing to the entire capital stock; $50,000, for instance, 30% of which must be paid in specie; one third of the stockholders must be residents. The banks could issue bank notes up to the amount of the capital stock. Many of the banks accepted a kind of paper denominated "specie certificates" which were deposited instead of specie. Others by pre-arrangements carried the specie deposit from one bank to another just ahead of the bank examiners. One specie deposit, therefore, served the purposes of several banks. Within a year, forty-nine banks were organized and within two years forty-two failed. Oakland County had the Bank of Kensington in the Southwest corner of the County capitalized at $50,000 in a village which had but twenty houses. The Bank of Sandstone with liabilities of $38,000 had no assets of any kind when it was examined and had never had any specie.

The Federal government had loaned millions of dollars to the states. President Andrew Jackson and his advisers understood the situation and knew that if the public lands could be paid for in bank notes the government would suffer a great loss. He therefore in 1836 issued his "specie circular" to the effect that the government would accept only silver and gold for its lands. The effect in Michigan was that the banks would accept only specie money. The bank notes became worthless. Business concerns couldn't borrow, they had to sell. "Land speculators by the thousands who purchased land and opened up town sites on canals, highways, railroads, and thought themselves rich, found their imaginary wealth evaporated and themselves poorer than when they entered the territory with barely means enough to make an opening in the wilderness." Not an honest working man or farmer in the state but had lost—some of them all they possessed—by these dishonest "wild cat" banks in Michigan. Charles lost no money in the bank failures as he had none to lose. He couldn't sell potatoes or wheat for silver or gold. The paper money was worth less than the German marks after the European war. He couldn't buy anything because he didn't have the silver. He traded potatoes for groceries. These were hard times experienced during the winter of 1837-1838. Many of the pioneers were reduced to the starvation point.

V

After the panic, came the fever and ague. On a beautiful warm day in June, Lewis and Charles L., who had been helping their father burn brush, came into the house shivering.

Lewis: "Ma, I am so cold!" His mother bundled him up in blankets and set him down by the warm fireplace. He shivered and shook until his teeth rattled. In half an hour the chill passed off and a fever set in and made him hot. The next day, Charles quit work at ten o'clock, came into the house, sat down by the fireplace next to the kettles and shook so hard that the dishes rattled and then he passed to the torrid zone. In the afternoon he went out to work again. The next day Lewis repeated and so did his father. Martha went up to the Smith's for advice. She described the symptoms.

Mrs. Smith: "That's the ague—chills and fever and sometimes sweats. All the settlers have it and nearly every season."

Martha: "Can the doctor cure it?"

Mrs. Smith: "No, he can't do much to relieve it. Quinine is the only medicine that will help."

Martha: "Does the child shake every day?"

Mrs. Smith: "The patient shakes at regular intervals. The chill comes on about the same hour every day or every other day as the case may be."

Martha: "Do ague patients ever die with it?"

Mrs. Smith: "Not often. Sometimes complications set in and make the patient very sick. After you get used to the ague you will plan on its coming and will sit down and wait for it, or go to bed and wrap the blankets about you when the time comes for you to "shake". The preacher appoints church service on the day he doesn't "shake". The judge holds court on the off days and the farmer arranges his work so he can sit before the fireplace and "shake" when his time comes."

Dr. J. M. Hoyt of Walled Lake was called. He said the chills and fever were due to decaying vegetation and that every body in this new country has it and for several years in succession, during the hot weather. The sickness had been so general that all the doctor's Peruvian bark had been used. His patients were so poor, because they were ill so much, that they couldn't pay the doctor for his services. He had no money for the purchase of quinine. He substituted for quinine a tea made from poplar or iron wood bark with good results for the patients.

The mosquitos were a pest, too; they bred in the nearby marsh. When Charles built a smudge back of the house to smoke the mosquitos, the oxen and cows would push into the smoke to get relief from their bites.

CHAPTER VI
CHARLES L.

I

There were two classes of pioneers who made trails to the Michigan territory. One was the promoter class not contented anywhere any length of time. The family would settle in Wayne County, for illustration, and when the neighbors began to encroach upon its view, the family would pull up and go west like Richard Garland did. The opportunities seemed better farther west even away out on the prairies of Illinois and Iowa. In this class possessed of the wanderlust was the pioneer who thought most money would be made by settling on a farm, making improvements then selling it to advantage. Then he would move farther inland and settle again.

The Hartsoughs, Stilsons, Murrays, Welfares, Severances belong to the other large class who went to Michigan to acquire lands, build homes and rear large, healthy families and were willing to make the necessary sacrifices to do it. They brought with them their religious convictions and helped to establish and support ministers and churches. They believed in education for their children and were willing to pay the "rate bills" and the taxes necessary for the building of school houses and for the employment of teachers. They came intending to stay: no thought of returning to the stony hills of New England nor even to the fruitful fields of western New York. They cut their bridges behind them. They valued a home above everything else—a home where they could live comfortably in their declining years—a home where they could rear a family of useful boys and girls who in turn would establish homes and repeat the processes. In the course of twenty years, Charles had developed a good farm free from indebtedness, had built a large white house which met the needs of his large family, and barns and outbuildings to care for his hay, grain, feed and to house his horses, oxen, cows, hogs, sheep, poultry. He was a prosperous farmer.

He and Martha reared a large family. After the Panic of 1837, Adelia was born, and in intervals of two or three years, Nathan, John, Jotham, and Elmina. The girls were assets to the mothers. They began young to wipe dishes, tidy up the house and do errands, and to help in a thousand other ways to relieve the mother of her many burdens. When the girls reached the teen age and before, they could do a large part of the housework allowing Martha to give time to spinning, knitting, weaving and making butter. It was a strenuous life for a well robust mother to make clothes and feed a family of eight growing boys and girls. Martha broke down under the burden. She enjoyed the new house only a few years. Considering the rough life of the pioneers and the exposure to which they were subjected and the diseases prevalent, Charles and

Martha were fortunate not to lose more than one child. Lewis, the first born in whom his father and mother took great delight, sickened and died at the age of fifteen. Surely a son was a very valuable economic asset to the early Michigan farmers. A boy could earn his keep at eleven or twelve years of age and could do a man's work from thirteen or fourteen years on. It was the custom which perhaps was sanctioned by law that the boy should work for his father until he became of age. In other words all his earnings belonged to his father. Charles had five boys working for him. Why should he not have cleared his farm, erected good buildings and have driven good horses?

The story of Charles L. is a story of boy life on the farm, the home life, the district school, the church and social customs. After he became a man, it is a story of farm life in Michigan and Illinois and of life in a typical Michigan village.

II

Charles L. was not an unusual child; was not precocious; had a good mind, learned readily; was full of mischief and enjoyed abundance of energy; loved good stories and practical jokes. He was democratic as all boys must be who are brought up on pioneer farms. His strenuous work on the farm developed seasoned muscles and great strength and endurance. He held his own in wrestling, boxing, and other boyish sports. He grew to be a stalwart man five feet, nine inches; well-built, sturdy, with a manly physique. His thick hair was black; his

MICHIGAN TRAILMAKERS 59

eyes were gray and dreamy; an expert with the axe and a crack shot with the rifle.

He belonged to the great middle class of our population. He was a representative of the pioneer farmers who settled the forests and prairies of Michigan, Illinois, and Wisconsin, and made this country a land of homes and villages where schools, churches, and orderly government were established and supported. The story of his aspirations, success and disappointments and defeats is typical of the men of the pioneer type who pushed westward the frontiers of civilization and inveigled the fields into the production of abundant crops of corn, oats, wheat, and potatoes.

At ten years of age, he cut down trees, trimmed the trunks and piled the brush. He drove the oxen hitched to the great iron-toothed drag which tore up the sod and leveled the soil for planting and sowing. He dropped corn and pumpkin seed in the hills and covered them with a hoe. As he grew older he went for the cow which had wandered into the woods, located her by the tinkling of the bell, fed the hogs and the chickens. He took his gun and guarded the corn field and hid behind a tree and shot the crows and the squirrels which dug up the seed corn just planted. He set traps for rabbits, for partridges and fox. He helped with the churning of the butter in the old dash church; and helped make soft soap by getting the barrel of wood ashes properly set so the water seeping through the ashes drained off into a bucket. It was then put into a large iron kettle to which was added pieces or refuse meat. He ran the hot tallow into the candle molds for his mother, chopped the meat into sausage and mixed up the meat and apples chopped for mince pies. On stormy days and winter evenings, he helped his mother clean and card the wool and wind the yarn. He kept the supply of wood by the fireplace and when he became strong enough he cut and hauled the back log to the door of the house, then with a cant hook rolled it into place, set the green wood andirons, rolled up the forestick and piled on the pitchy tamarack wood. He took wheat to the grist mill at Farmington. He mounted the horse and sat on top the bag of wheat which was just full enough to allow the grain in either end of the sack to balance over the backbone of the horse. In the early spring, he had the pleasure of making wooden spiggots, driving them into an augur hole he bored into the hard maple, and of watching the drip drip of the sweet sap into the buckets and then the boiling down of the sap and of tasting the maple syrup and maple sugar. It was great sport for him and Lewis to locate a bee tree and to secure their winter's honey, and to discover trees which would make good ox yokes or good ax helves.

He was not unacquainted with digging and picking up potatoes, and in picking and housing the apples,—greenings, spitzenbergen, northern spies, seek-no-furthers, and russets, and cider making in the home-made mill with grinders and pressers.

In his early teens he was as good as a man for the lighter work; in his later teens no man in the neighborhood could outdo him. When he was not in

MICHIGAN TRAILMAKERS

school in the winter he was felling trees and splitting oak rails for the zigzag rail fence of his day. He knew how to stand and how to strike to make the ax eat into the oak trunk. Every stroke counted. After the tree fell, the stump showed an even surface almost as smooth as the saw would leave it, he was so skillful with his ax.

On one occasion Alonzo one of Charles L.'s chums came over in the morning to go fishing at the lake with Charles. His father was very strict about letting his sons off a day for sports, such as fishing. When the boys asked him for permission to go he replied giving them a stunt: "You may go after you have cut and corded two and a half cords of four foot wood." They accepted the challenge. Charles chopped and Alonzo corded two and a half cords of wood by four o'clock, but they were too weary to go fishing after that.

He learned wood craft, the age of trees, by concentric rings. He knew the names of the trees, the basswood, beach, birch, poplars, cedars, tamarack, the hard and soft maples, the hickory and the elm. He got acquainted with the squirrels, the deer, the coon, the opossum, the quail, wild turkey, and wild duck, the partridge, crows, hawks, turkey buzzards, black bass, rock bass, pickerel, roach, perch, sunfish, and bullheads. He could read the secrets of the skies and tell when rain or snow would come, when the weather would be fair, "a rainbow at night, sailors delight," and the like.

Boys, dressed in woolen suits, coonskin caps, heavy woolen mittens and cowhide boots over woolen socks, can stand lots of cold, but when the thermometer indicated sub-zero weather, watering the stock in a creek half a mile away was not a warm job. He drove the oxen, horses, and cows to the creek to water and cut holes in the ice. After filling up on ice water, the cows humped up their backs, hair standing on end and shivered, but he frosted his fingers and ears and toes and consequently suffered from chilblains the rest of the winter. A heavy fall of drifting snow in the winter frequently covered the house and barn so that all one could see of the house was the chimney where the hot smoke escaped. Then he tugged against the door to get it open and tunnelled under the snow to the barn to reach the stock. The great snow drifts on the north and south road in front of the house made the roads impassable. The family was snowbound for days.

III

In Charles L.'s later teen years, haying and harvesting furnished the heaviest work of the year. The farmer hurried to get his hay in before it should rain. To pitch hay upon the wagon and from the wagon to the stack or hay mow required the energy and strength of the most sturdy young men. Swinging the cradle all day in wheat harvest was still more strenuous. There was no part of the harvesting Charles L. enjoyed more than binding the bundles, dropped by the McCormick reaper. It required three men to keep up with the machine and a fourth to shock the bundles. The early machine drawn by horses or oxen was constructed "with a reel to throw the standing grain upon the platform back of the vibrating sickles and its huge rake which rose at regular intervals like a great red beckoning hand, swept through the air with an ingenious and effective twist and swept the sheaf into a gavel which lay beside its track, a most impressive and picturesque tool." The binders were stationed one-third the way around the field. The first started after the machine, pulled from the sheaf bound enough straw to bind the next. As he walked he twisted it into form, the heads in the middle, the butts spread, his thumb on the crooked back of the heads. As he approached the gavel and his feet shoved the grain up into a sheaf, he dexterously squared it up with a single toss, threw the band about it as he lifted it, laid it on the ground as he cinched it up and tucked the straw into a knot. Then he threw it away, at the same time snatching out the straw for the next. At the end of his station where the man ahead of him had begun, his shirt was dripping with sweat as he looked back for the oncoming reaping machine.

Hog killing time came in the fall when a year's supply of pork was put down for the winter. Several hogs were killed at a time and spare ribs sent to the neighbors while the side pork, hams and shoulders were salted and cured and smoked in the smoke-house, with hickory limbs and bark. By study and practice, Charles L. became expert at sticking a hog. The hog was caught, turned over on his back feet up. While his father held the legs,

Charles L. put his left hand on the snout and pressing down, with the right hand, he pushed the sharp knife blade into the hog's throat and with a slight twist of the hand severed the jugular vein. The hog was allowed to roll back and get upon his feet while the blood gurgled as it ran out through the wound. A boiler full of hot water was carried from the kitchen stove and emptied into a large rain barrel which was propped against a platform of planks on saw horses, so that the edge of the barrel was on a level with the plank floor. With a skid and a hog hook the men drew the hog up head first upon the platform and pushed the hog into the barrel of hot water hind end first to scald him so the hairs would slip off easily. After pulling up and letting down the carcass into the hot water it was drawn out upon the platform and by use of scrapers made for the purpose, and butcher knives, the hair was soon removed from the back end of the hog. Then the carcas was reversed with the same operation. After cleaning the hog, a two foot stick sharp at either end was inserted into the gambrel joints by which the carcas was hung against a tree in position for dressing. After the inwards were removed, the carcas was split from feet to head in the middle. Then it was cut up into hams, shoulders, side pork, rib roasts, etc.

After the fall plowing was over and the "frost was on the pumpkin and the corn was in the shock," husking had to be done. The corn was cut with a sickle or corn cutter while there was a little greenness in the stalks and leaves. The stalks after husking were stacked in the barnyard and fed to the stock during the winter months. Husking the corn was the last of the fall's work, and sometimes snow covered the shocks before the work was done and the corn safely stowed away in the corn crib. Charles L. made a husking peg by whittling out a hickory peg about four or five inches long coming to a sharp point at one end. The peg had buckskin straps fastened to it so that the strap would cover the two middle fingers which allowed the sharp point to project about an inch over the fore finger when the peg was grasped in the hand with the two middle fingers through the strap. The point was used to pierce the husk and tear it from the corn. He sat on his knees with the stalks lying on the ground in front of him with the tassels to his right. As fast as the ears were husked and broken from the stalks and thrown into a pile the stalks were pushed back under his knees until he got enough for a bundle when he would tie it up with a tough stalk or a willow withe. When the piles of husked corn were picked up and loaded in the wagon box, it showed that Charles averaged seventy-five to eighty bushels of ears of red nose corn a day.

IV

The early settlers in Oakland County were from New England and New York where they inherited the tradition of education in the home and in district schools, covering reading, writing, spelling, arithmetic. Within a few years after Charles's settlement in the county a school district was formed which embraced the Greenes, Murrays, Stilsons, Phelps, Severances, and some others north and south, and called the Greene district. A log school house was soon erected built on the order of log houses. It had a front door on wooden hinges and the leather latch string, windows on the sides with panes fastened and held in place by wooden pegs. The desks were boards running the length of the room, laid on pegs driven into the logs about three feet from the floor. The seats were made by driving wooden legs into boards or slabs and by placing the seats parallel to the desks. The pupils therefore sat facing the walls as there were no seats in the middle of the room. There was a large fireplace in the back end; the teacher's desk in the front end. The teacher rapped on the window to call the children in for school. There were no blackboards, no steel pens, no slates, no lead pencils. Pens were made from goose quills, turkey, and turkey buzzard quills. Lewis and Charles used unruled writing paper, but had a "rule and plummet," a piece of lead in the shape of a narrow and much elongated wedge for ruling the paper. They used Webster's Elementary Spelling Book, a curious and interesting old speller. The first pages contained an analysis of sounds, with a key, and the alphabet followed by words in columns to be spelled followed by sentences containing the words so pupils could get the meaning and pronunciation of words. Then followed words of two syllables, words of three syllables and so on. There were four fables and three stories with morals,— the dog, the stag, the squirrel. The book closed with a long list of sentences containing words pronounced alike but spelled differently, such as "rain", "rein", "road", "rode". The English reader was Lindley Murray's. It contained a "selection from the best writers designed to assist young persons to read with propriety and effect; to improve their language and sentiments and to inculcate some of the most important principles of piety and virtue". The selections include such selections as "Cataract of Niagara" by Goldsmith. "Apostle Paul's Noble Defense Before Festus and Agrippa"—Bible—Acts. "Nightingale and Glowworm" (poetry) by Cowper. "On Pride" (poetry) by Pope. "The Morning in Summer" (poetry) by Thomson.

The English Reader was superseded by the McGuffy Readers which were used forty or fifty years. The other books were Olney's Geography and Doball's Arithmetic.

Charles was a good speller. He mastered the old "blue backed" speller and practiced spelling down until he mastered all the words in the book. He learned many of the selections in the English Reader and particularly the stories and the histories.

The district schools made a specialty of spelling. The Hosner School, three miles north and east of the Greene School, confident that their spellers were superior to those spellers in the Greene School challenged them. The Greene School accepted the challenge and drilled every day for the event. The schools met at the Hosner School House on a frosty moonlight night in January. Both districts were well represented. It was an event similar in interest to our football games and was a real social event. On the Hosner side were the Forbushes, Andrewses, Bachelors, Hosners. On the Greene side the Murrays, Stilsons, Phelps, Severances. The line of spellers extended around two sides and one end of the room. The teacher of the Hosner School presided and pronounced the words. Easy words first then he launched into polysyllables,—separate, transmigrate, government, Presbyterian. Very soon only six on a side were left standing, then came subsidiary, unnecessary, heterogeneous and Charles was standing alone having won for the Greene School. Among the Hosner girls who came forward to congratulate him was a striking black haired girl with bright sparkling eyes. She made a strong impression on Charles. Charles L. was fond of arithmetic, particularly the practical problems which he solved in "his head", as the expression went, without "figgering" with quill and paper or crayon and paper.

Charles L. loved to trap and to hunt. He had traps set in the woods which he could reach by a detour on his way to school. He told me the following story:

"One morning, I found a skunk in my trap but he was dead. I skinned him, put the skin in my pocket and hurried to school. I rushed up to the fireplace to get warm. With the warming, the odor of skunk was apparent. The boys held their noses, the girls shied away. The teacher followed his long sensitive nose to me. The skunk was thrown out, and I had to stand for a half hour with a string tied to each thumb and attached to a peg high enough up on the side wall to make me stand with hands raised as high as my chin and held there. Gosh! it was a severe punishment."

He told also of an exercise in expression. Three boys in the class were drilling in reading, "The wind of a hundred years have whistled through my branches". Alonzo and Alfred could say the lines with proper emphasis but William made a mess of it. He was slow to comprehend. He read "The—winds—of—a—hundred years whist—whist—led—through my—breeches".

"Boarding round" was a hardship on teachers but the custom obtained in the Greene District as late as 1888. The teacher had the fires to build and frequently the wood to furnish and cut,—all for $12.00 to $15.00 a month which was raised by the rate bill prior to 1850. Children were assessed pro rata on the number of days attendance at school. So many of the boys had to work in the fall and in the spring that school was kept only three months in a year.

Education in the home was mostly practical. Children were taught to do things and handle tools. In most homes the Bible, the almanac, the Detroit Free Press, were the materials of culture. Martha taught her children to read the Bible and explained the meanings. The Sunday School supplemented her teaching. The Detroit Free Press was read constantly which may account for Charles L's knowledge of contemporary events such as the building of railroads, plank roads, the slavery agitation and other political events.

He read and reread the dark blue covered patent medicine almanac which hung in an honored place on a peg near the fireplace or on a nail behind the kitchen door. As a little boy he pitied the man on the front cover whose vitals were opened for inspection and had arrows pointing to the vital parts with names of the Zodiac at the outer ends of the arrows. What did "Aries" and "Taurus" and "Pisces" have to do with healing and with curing this unfortunate man? He turned to the pages to find out what the weather would be tomorrow and on Friday night when the spelling match was to occur; and he read: "Allen's Cherry Pectoral to purify the blood, Hood's Sarsaparilla for the blood" and the endorsement of their curative properties by names of men and women who may have lived at the ends of the earth as far as he was concerned, who had been helped or cured. He loved the aphorisms, such as "after dinner rest a while, after supper run a mile."

He read his text books at home and committed to memory many selections from the English Reader such as the "Nightingale and the Glowworm". In later life, he was an assiduous reader.

V

Religion was a large factor in the lives of the settlers in this community as it had been in their lives in New England. The church meetings were social as well as religious. Rev. Caleb Lamb wrote that women with babes in arms would follow the trail for four or five miles to enjoy a religious meeting. Wherever there were a few Christian families in a community there was occasional preaching. The preachers were either circuit riders of the Methodist Church or Missionary preachers of the Baptist denomination. The New York Baptist convention sent missionaries into Michigan of whom the best known were the Rev. Nehemiah Lamb and his son, Caleb, mentioned in Chapter I. On his first trip in 1824, Nehemiah preached in Pontiac, the only Baptist Church in Oakland County. He then preached to a company at Stony Point and organized a church, and at Troy where another church was organized. He preached in other communities where a few families could be assembled in a home or in a school house. Caleb came to Michigan to live in 1829 under appointment from the New York Baptist Convention and went from settlement to settlement preaching and organizing churches one of which was the little church at West Farmington where Charles and Martha were members.

The Methodist Missionaries were early in the field riding circuits and caring for the spiritual welfare of the pioneers. The little group in the Bachelor neighborhood was served by a circuit rider from Farmington who held services in the Hosner school house. The few Methodists in the village of Walled Lake, received the ministration of the Circuit rider from Farmington at first, then from the circuit rider of the Commerce circuit.

CHAPTER VII
THE FORBUSHES

It frequently happened in the early settlement of Michigan that people of the same nationality and kinfolks took up farms from the government and settled in the same community, frequently on adjacent farms. German settlements in Illinois, Swedish settlements in Minnesota, Norwegian settlements, similar to the settlements in South Dakota described by Rolvaag in his "Giants of the Earth" were all duplicated in Michigan. The Scots settled about Orchard and Pine Lakes in Oakland County. Kinfolk frequently settled in the same community where they were able to secure farms adjacent or not far apart; such was the case of the Bachelors, Orrs, Hosners, Forbushes who settled about three miles south of Orchard Lake in West Bloomfield township and four miles east of Charles Severance's farm, and a few miles west of Birmingham.

When the tide of immigration set in from Western New York, Consider Bachelor and his family were borne in on the flood tide. There were Samuel and Sidney with their families; Susan and William Orr and little Frank; Hannah and Thomas Hosner and Martin Van Buren; Julia and Ed. Allan; Catherine and Edwin Forbush and their daughter, Lyvonia, and sons Henry and Cordon; and Abbey Bachelder

MICHIGAN TRAILMAKERS 73

and her husband. They took up farms on either side of the highway which runs directly west from Birmingham. In the same district was John Andrews, William Coe, and Seeley Harger for whom the first school house was named. Edwin was a native of Massachusetts, the son of Bliss Forbush, a farmer and shoemaker who might have traced his lineage back to France through England. Bliss emigrated to western New York early in the century when the New England states became congested with population and farmers heard that good land free from stones was to be had in New York. Edwin, his son, born in 1805, married Catherine Bachelor and settled on a farm in Clarkson, Cayuga County, New York. After the Bachelors settled in West Bloomfield they wrote in such effulgent praise of the great opportunities in Michigan, of the climate, of the soil, of the forests and the possibilities of homes for themselves and their children, that the lure of the west became so strong that Edwin sold out and settled near Samuel in 1832. Edwin and Catherine purchased one hundred and sixty acres of wood land from the government in the timbered hills and valleys west of Hosner school house in West Bloomfield, built a regulation size and style of log house, such as has been described earlier in this book and settled with their three children, Lyvonia, Cordon and Henry, two years before Charles settled in Commerce township. Edwin was an industrious man and managed to save sufficient money made off his New York farm to pay for his Michigan land and his expenses until he could raise a crop. By the time

Charles arrived in Farmington the Bachelor settlement showed many acres of cleared and productive land and a school house where the "circuit rider" often held religious services, named the Harger School at first, but later the Hosner School in honor of Thomas Hosner.

The soil was light clay well drained but Edwin soon discovered that the clay soil must not be plowed or cultivated when it was wet. The story of the clearing of the farm, erecting good buildings, the sowing, planting, reaping, threshing, the hard times, and the panic of 1837 are replicas of the story of Charles's pioneer life and do not need repeating. Cordon and Henry furnished man power for the development of the farm.

After twelve years work, Edwin still lived in the original log house. He erected a barn for his oxen, horses, and cows in which to keep them warm. He had pig sties, sheep cotes, but the same old house, the same old fireplace, the old cranes and kettles, and bedsteads. The boys, thirteen and fifteen years of age still slept on their ticks of cornhusk or straw on the second floor. Pioneer farmers and modern farmers for the most part emphasized the value of hogs and cows and minimized the value of housewives, and children. The legislature of the present age will more quickly appropriate money for the extermination of the foot and mouth disease, and for the destruction of the corn borer than for the eradication of the hook worm and tuberculosis.

Catherine was an exceptional woman in that she was strong and robust and could endure the strenuous work and assume the responsibilities of the house, of rearing children (she had already given birth to eight), of clothing the family by weaving and sewing and knitting, of providing food for the family, early breakfasts and late suppers. She gloried in her strength and her ability to turn off work. She was happy with her family; Henry, a freckled faced boy of fifteen, a promising lad who some day would have a farm near theirs; Cordon, a robust and sturdy boy of thirteen years; her eldest girl, Louisa, nearly twelve, a bright, active little girl with hazel eyes and black hair, a picture of her mother. Then came Lavancha, four years old, Mabel, two years old, and Edwin, less than a year old. She rejoiced in her growing family and in Edwin and in the home they were building. She was happy, also, in having brothers and sisters near her. On holidays and Sunday, the families were together. Her nephews, Mack Bachelor and Martin Van Buren Hosner and Francis Orr were rapidly growing out of youth into manhood. When all the families assembled at the Forbushes, the boys would play fox and geese and sham battle with snow balls in the winter time, and broad jump, run and jump and foot races in the summer time. When middle life for Catherine was so sweet and enjoyable, death came stalking by. She was taken sick on Monday and died the following Sunday with erysipelas in 1845. They interred the body in the cemetery at North Farmington.

"What would Edwin do for a housekeeper?" was asked by the neighbors of one another. Edwin asked himself the question and answered "No girls in the neighborhood to be had. We will get along somehow."

Many years later Louisa told her children the story of the years following her mother's death. She said: "Aunt Ann and Aunt Susan told Pa that they would help me all they could and Pa told me that the boys would help with the work in the house when the responsibility of the home fell upon my shoulders. I lacked two months of being twelve years old. I was well and strong and as full of energy as a young colt and I set to with a will. Eddie was only eleven months' old and needed the constant care of a mother to feed and clothe and keep him clean. Pa fed him at the table and took him to bed with him. Lavancha, only four years old, needed help and care instead of having to help me with the work. Henry and Cordon had grown to youth without learning how to wipe dishes, make beds and carry water for cooking. The glamour of my task vanished in a few weeks. The hard work of lifting the heavy kettles and hanging them on the crane, preparing potatoes and cooking bread in the bake oven and getting meals on the table for our family of six was more than I could stand up under. Aunt Hannah helped for several weeks in getting the bread ready for the bake kettle and helped with the washing. Housekeeping in a log house and cooking over a fireplace is no comparison to the ease and comfort of a modern home with its cook stove and its heater, and with utensils handy. I went up the ladder and threw myself down on the cornhusk tick at night with my feet aching, my shoulders and legs aching and the muscles twitching and cried myself to sleep. It seemed no time before I heard Pa calling before daylight, "Time to get up".

"Do you see how my shoulders droop? Round shoulders due to lifting heavy pails, lifting and caring for Eddie. Only a strong physique and courage and spirit and a keen sense of duty kept me to my task. As the years went by and I grew stronger and Eddie became able to help himself and Lavancha became helpful, the burdens became easier and the responsibilities less irksome. Then a dreadful thing happened. Cordon at eighteen years of age, and industrious boy helping about the house, nearly old enough to start a home of his own, stepped on a rusty nail and was maimed for life. He never used the foot again. He walked on crutches and knitted mittens at fifty cents a pair and other jobs which he could do with his hands."

"The district school was only half a mile from our house. What time could I get to go to school after getting Lavancha, Mabel and Eddie ready and after doing my house work? I went to school before Mother died and learned to read and to write and to do sums in arithmetic. My education was very practical. No girl of my acquaintance could care for a home better than I could. We went to church held in the school house occasionally at first and then regularly by one of those "circuit riders" and occasionally we drove to the Baptist Church at North Farmington. I loved the service and have always loved those old hymns we used to sing and frequently now hum or sing 'The promised land'."

This little settlement was greatly stirred by the news of the discovery of gold in California in 1848. General Kit Carson brought several nuggets of gold with him in 1848 on his trip to Washington to report to headquarters. The covered wagon train bound for Oregon in 1848 detoured at Fort Bridger for California when the news of gold first reached it. Travellers coming east brought the news. The newspapers with their bold headlines flashed the news over the country so that early in 1849, thousands of gold seekers from the east and middlewest set out for California overland in caravans of hundreds of wagons, and by ship to Panama, and by foot or ox carts across to the Pacific coast and then after waiting two months or three months, they got ships for San Francisco where the ships were abandoned. Engineers, firemen, deckhands—all bought shovels, picks, tin pans, cooking utensils and went northeast to Sutter's landing.

The boys in the Bachelor neighborhood were eager to start west at once. The fathers and mothers were fearful of what might befall their sons who had never been farther than twenty miles from home. They had seen Detroit, but California was on the other side of the world. Little groups of the boys and groups of men at church discussed the proposition pro and con.

Edwin said: "It is a mighty dangerous trip overland and besides the distance is so great you could never walk it."

MICHIGAN TRAILMAKERS 79

Samuel: "Yes and if you should ride one of our fine horses and he should die on the way, what would you do stranded on the western plains where the Indians would hunt your scalp and the vultures would wait for your body and the body of the horse, and besides it would require a lot of gold to pay for the horse."

Thomas: "The whole world of adventurers will be there before you and you might not strike a vein of gold at all. Then where would you be and how would you get back?"

William: "I say, boys, I wouldn't go. We have good farms here, you all have excellent opportunities to make good homes and a comfortable living."

The mothers shed tears and begged their sons not to think of going, but Henry had no mother. He was of age, twenty-one, had no one dependent upon him, was free to take a chance of finding gold enough to make him rich. He was a freckled faced lad, solidly built, reddish brown hair, with an embryo beard of the same color. He stood about five feet high, a clean frank face, goodness and tenderness shone in his mild eyes. His face radiated hope and kindness. His square chin indicated decision, determination and courage. It was arranged that a young man near Farmington would be his companion. Then came the excitement of getting ready for the long journey. Louisa made him a knapsack for food and for the little things he might wish to carry, such as needles, yarn, etc. and consecrated the sack with briny tears. Two new shirts, an extra pair of pants and socks were included. The whole neighborhood was at church Sunday to see him and wish him a safe journey and good luck. Monday, after tearful and sorrowful farewells, his father took Henry to Detroit where he met George. The boys took train for Chicago where they got into a train of schooners bound for Independence, Missouri, the assembling point of caravans from the north, east, and south, preparatory for the two thousand miles of prairie, desert, mountains and fertile valleys en route to the land of gold. The covered wagons took one of three routes to the Pacific. Henry and George fell in with a party going overland by way of Bennet's Point, Denver, Salt Lake City and San Francisco—the route now traversed by the Union Pacific Railway. At San Francisco, the boys purchased blankets, a few cooking utensils, some food, a pick, a shovel, and a tin pan at $5.00 each and followed the crowd to the gold mines. Then followed the hard work of digging in the creek bottoms and washing the ore, while they stood ankle deep in the cold icy mountain stream. There were shallow excavations and construction of washing bins—a long summer of hard work, but lots of gold dust as a reward. The boys were cautious and sensible. The large amount of gold acquired didn't make them reckless. They avoided the gambling dens where other miners lost in an hour all of their output for the summer months and were stranded and compelled to stay for the next year or become moral and economic derelicts. Henry and George buckled around them their specially constructed leather belts filled with gold dust, with pistols and cartridges protruding from the belt in front. They wore the belts continuously on their voyage down the Pacific Coast across the Isthmus of Panama, then by ship to New York and by train to Detroit where they arrived on an early spring afternoon. The frequenters of the Detroit hotel, where they intended to stay over night were curious and unduly interested in these returned '49ers.

Henry to George: "Did you see that fellow look at us askance? I don't like his looks. Let's go."

George: "For home?"

Henry: "Yes. We are safer on the road than we are here if we can steal away, and keep our powder dry."

Aided by the brightness of the full moon in a cloudless sky, they left the highway and followed woodland trails and reached home at one o'clock in the morning.

CHAPTER VIII
CHARLES L. WINS A BRIDE
I

Farm life in every community would be dull, monotonous, and depressing were it not for the few occasions when neighbor visits neighbor and members of the community meet together in church worship, in socials and picnics, at quilting bees, at threshing bees, logging bees, house and barn raisings and grain threshing in the fall of the year. A favorite outing was the annual spring and the annual fall trips to town, when the whole family would go together on a load of grain or on a load of poultry or on a load of potatoes. There were butter and eggs to be sold, groceries to be purchased, shoes and boots and clothes to be fitted to the whole family. It was a social event, a real outing for the housewives, especially. The growing city of Pontiac was the trade center of Oakland County. It boasted of a railroad and an improved highway running directly to Detroit, the metropolis and trade center of the state.

The school house in the Bachelor community was a social center. The children gathered here for school, the whole community for the spelling matches and for the preaching once or twice a month. The worship together and the preaching gave the people an uplift and furnished new ideals and inspirations. Such services transferred the every day thoughts into new channels. They made life seem more worth while. On these occasions, the women chatted about their hats and dresses, about chickens, butter and eggs, about their ailments if they were unfortunate enough to have them, and about their babies and boys and girls. The men swapped horses, and sold seed potatoes and seed wheat and talked about the prospects of crops, of rain, and of dry weather and its effects upon crops. After a Sunday off like this, the farmer and his wife and the boys and girls all started the work on Monday with new vigor and renewed energy.

Threshing time was an event of the season. The women folk looked forward eagerly for the day which would bring all the neighbors together. The neighbor women would come in and help prepare the big dinner. The boys and girls loved the hustle of the threshers, and their banter and jokes and stories. They loved to see the horses go round and round and hear the whir and the purr of the swift cylinder.

The grain was now, in the fifties, cut with the reaper, bound by hand, shocked, and drawn to the barnyard and stacked. After standing in the stack for a month or six weeks to season it was threshed. Seeley Harger's thresher, which did not separate the straw and chaff from the grain, and for which the power was furnished by the treadmill operated by horse power, had been superseded by the big thresher which carried the straw to the stack and winnowed the grain by an attached fanning mill.

Henry remained at home during the summer to help with the work as Cordon was too badly crippled even to run the mower or reaper. He located a farm during the summer and purchased it with his California gold, a farm located in a pleasant valley with high hills on two sides, about four miles west of the town of Milford. It was a beautiful valley with rich soil formed from the erosion of the hill sides.

Henry and his father, Edwin, followed the thresher through the neighborhood and beyond, including the Severances, and by a tradition of exchange of labor, earned enough time for manning the thresher for their own grain. They finished the season at the Forbushes. Henry came home from the Andrewses where the threshing was just finished. He said to Louisa: "The threshers will be here tonight!" Eddie overheard, shouted "Goodie", and ran out to the road to see if they were in sight, then climbed the rail fence. That wasn't high enough, then he scaled the side of the house and stood upon the roof ridge looking west toward the Andrewses. Finally he saw the great thresher coming. "Whoopee". Then quickly he slid off the roof, rushed across the yard and ran up the road. He rode back perched high upon the machine behind his cousin Mack.

The separator was drawn up between the stack of oats and the stack of wheat with the straw carrier pointing to the stack of straw to be made. The wheels were sunk three or four inches in the ground so the vibration of the separator would not move the machine. The "power" was drawn into place and spiked down by lantern light. The turkey gobbler roosting high in the tree near the barn aroused his harem and in turkey language put them on guard and cheered them with his courageous gobble. The chickens in the trees sensed something wrong and began cackling, climbing higher and the rooster alternately soothed his flock and crowed to keep up his courage. The geese in the barn lot surprised at this strange phenomena rent the air with their hisses and raucous cries. The colts in the adjacent meadow approached cautiously, took a look, snorted, turned about and with heads high and curved necks, galloped off to the far end of the field.

Edwin caught three young cockerels in the hen house, wrung their necks and dressed them, singed them, cut them up ready for the pot. Louisa and Lavancha pared a great pan of potatoes by candlelight, set the bread to rise with emptyings so that it would be ready for the bake oven in the morning.

The next morning before the break of day the cocks began to crow and the gobbler to strut and the geese to scold, which awakened the men from their heavy slumbers. They were soon out to milk the cows, feed the horses and harness them, to feed the pigs and to pile wood around the fireplace. Seeley and Mack examined the thresher, drove additional spikes into the ground to hold the "power", adjusted the leather bands, made ready the table to catch the bundles and the platform for the band cutter, elevated the straw carrier into place, connected the tubes and the spout for carrying the grain and set the measures in place to receive it. The early sun gave promise of a clear day. The haze of early morning gave way to a clear sky with gray clouds racing across it. The frost was on the pumpkin and on the cold west wind, but he was soon overcome by the warm rays of the sun and left in the shade.

Eddie was down at daylight. You couldn't keep a lively kid like Eddie in bed when the threshers were there. He bolted out the door to the thresher and called back: "There comes Uncle Sam and Uncle Will with their teams, and Cousin Frank". Looking toward the east he shouted: "Uncle Thomas and Cousin Van with their gray horses."

"Got enough men to run the machine, Cousin Mack?"

Mack: "No, not yet. We expect the Severance boys and Johnnie and Lish".

He looked to the west and saw three horsemen galloping toward him. He soon discerned Charles L., Chalkley and Johnnie, and to the north across the field came Elisha Farmer. Mack was a fat, robust young man who took life easy and moderate, never got in a hurry, apt to choose the easiest jobs. It may have been this reason that gave him the job of driving the horses to furnish the power. The "power" was staked to the ground several feet from the thresher. It consisted of a lot of cog wheels. The ends of the sweeps were attached here; a large square platform was placed on top on which the driver sat or stood; a tumbling rod fastened together with a special contrivance called knuckle joints was attached at one end to the "power" the other to some cogs which ran the cylinder of the thresher into which the grain was fed. The four teams were hitched each to the end of a sweep with the bridle strap attached to the end of the sweep in front. The horses furnished the power to turn the cog wheels and this power was transferred to the cylinder by the tumbling rod which lay spiked down by collars close to the ground so the horses could step over the turning rod without injury.

Mack mounted the platform above the "power," carrying a long whip stalk in his hand to which was attached a short rawhide lash. The off horse was therefore near enough to the driver to feel the cut of the whip lash. Seeley stood before the great cylinder ready to feed the grain into its greedy mow. Van stood next with the serrated band knife in his hand ready to cut the bands. Charles L. and Elisha mounted the stack ready to throw bundles. Edwin and Frank stood ready to catch the golden grain and bag it while Sam and Thomas stood at the end of the carrier to receive the straw.

Seeley shouted to Mack: "Let her go."

Mack flourished his whip: "Come on boys," "get up there, Bill", "heave to", "The day's begun", "Come Jack, get into your collar." The horses began to pull, the wheels began to move, the tumbling rod began to tumble, the great wheel that turned the cylinder began to whirl and the deep bass voice of the cylinder began to sing and its deafening song could be heard for miles. The more rapidly the wheel turned, the more nearly like a purr became the whir of the cylinder. When the tune reached the right pitch, Seeley caught a bundle with his right hand, spread it out and fed it evenly into the cylinder. A steady stream of bundles poured upon the feeding table, the bands were cut by Van, the grain fed into the machine by Seeley, the straw fell from the carrier upon the stack. Edwin and Frank caught the wheat in measures, emptied it into bags which were carried by William to the granary and emptied.

Eddie wanted to be a thresher so he could feed the grain. In his eyes that was the big job, the most important one. "When I grow up," he told Lavancha, "I am going to be thresher man and feed the bundles of grain into the great cylinder." Then he looked at Mack who seemed to be so comfortably sitting on the box above the "power" with nothing to do but to keep the horses walking at the proper speed, and thought, "I'd like that job." Just then the west wind rushed him; he saw Mack slapping his sides with his arms and hands to get them warm; he ran around the stack for shelter. Then he rushed out to help Uncle Sam stack the straw, got dust in his eyes, nose and throat, then slid off the stack and went to watch the stream of wheat pulsing out the spout and running into the measure. A miracle: "Where does it come from?" "The bundles of grain pushed into the top of the machine; the wheat coming out here, and the straw carried to the stack."

About ten o'clock, Seeley gave way to Johnnie Andrews and Chalk changed places with Van and cut bands. Then Thomas, black with dirt, his white

MICHIGAN TRAILMAKERS

teeth shining like a negro's, yelled from the straw stack: "Give us some straw, Johnnie." Charles L. shouted back: "We will cover you up," and made the bundles fly. Mack cracked his whip and yelled to the steaming horses. The sleepy growl of the cylinder rose to a howl and the wheat came pulsing out the spout in such a stream that William carrying the grain, shouts to Johnnie: "Hold up, you will have the wheat all over the ground."

Aunt Susan and Aunt Hannah came over early and were in the kitchen helping Louisa get dinner for the threshers. The table was set, the dinner cooked in the great kettles hanging to the cranes in the fireplace. At twelve o'clock Eddie ran out of the house and shouted in his slender voice "Dinner," but no one heard him. Then he ran to his father, who backed away from the measures of wheat, and shouted in a loud voice "Dinner!"

Mack called to his horses: "Whoa! Whoa there boys! Steady Bill! Slow up Jack!" and held the whip stalk out in front of their eyes to convince them that he really meant them to stop. He jumped down, released the traces and each owner hustled to get his team to water and to feed. Charles and Van slid off the stack of grain, Sam and Thomas rolled off the straw and they all ran to the wash basin just outside the house so as to be the first to get washed and seated at the dinner table.

In the center of the table in front of Edwin was the large platter of steaming potatoes pared ready for mashing. On either side of the platter were smaller platters of boiled chicken, cut ready to serve, plates of bread at either end of the table. Just to the right of Edwin almost in front of Johnnie was the large bowl of hot chicken gravy with biscuits swimming in it. Johnnie was a devout Methodist and when he asked the blessing at the table he had the habit of bending forward, dropping his face within an inch or two of his plate. Edwin nodded to him to ask the blessing; Charles, who sat next to Edwin, moved the bowl of gravy and biscuits in front of Johnnie at the very moment when his head dropped forward. His nose dropped into the hot soup. He started to say "Our Father—" and ended with, "Gosh darn it! It's hot!" to the great amusement of all the men. The whole table was in an uproar. They liked practical jokes. Louisa poured the coffee and kept the cups filled, and passed the cream and sugar. Lavancha filled other cups with water. Aunt Susan and Aunt Hannah kept the chicken, potatoes, gravy, bread and butter moving. The men set to with a will as they did with their work. They were ravenously hungry. By the time they reached the dessert—the gingerbread—they became talkative and chafed the young men about their girls. Van, who was "shining up" to the Dye girl over South, told about a neighbor who had been annoyed by Dye's chickens and who killed two of them, and served a dinner to which he invited the Dyes. When Ezekiel was full of chicken and was praising its quality and the cooking of it, his friend told him that the chicken should be good as it was one of his (Dye's) own raising. Others talked about crops. Samuel told William that his corn would go one hundred bushels of ears to the acre. Edwin said his wheat would yield about fifty bushels to the acre.

Edwin: "Are you fattening any steers, Charles?" "Yes, twenty head. Indications are the prices will be high in January."

William to Johnny: "How much wheat did you sow?"

Johnny: "Thirty acres. It is already up, looks fine."

They all praised Louisa and Lavancha for their bountiful dinner. Louisa, now seventeen, was an efficient, capable, housekeeper and cook. As she and her sister moved about the table serving, the young bachelors were properly impressed. As Louisa stood by the fireplace after the dessert was served, with arms akimbo, with her new apron on, sleeves rolled up to her elbows, sparkling eyes and beaming face, having a feeling of satisfaction that her dinner was appreciated and enjoyed, she looked good and wholesome, efficient, attractive, the embodiment of every quality which might be found in the ideal girl and wife. She was particularly attractive to Charles L., who had thoughts of making a home. When he observed Louisa in her role of housekeeper and ate her delicious dinner,—the hot, crisp biscuits, the chicken done to the king's taste—he found the solution of his problem. While pitching bundles to the feeder in the afternoon he became listless, his mind seemed to wander. It wasn't centered on his pitching bundles. He was building aircastles for the future.

Seeley would call out, "Wake up, Charles, are you sick?"

After dinner Seeley and Samuel mended the fan belt, oiled the cogs in the "power" and in the cylinder and the wheels of the carrier so that the machine would be ready when the call, "One o'clock" should come. The boys did the hop, skip and jump, during the noon hour. They even got up a wrestling match between Charles L. and Francis. When the threshers finished at night and left for their homes, Henry said to Charles L.: "Come over some time and I will tell you about my trip to California." Charles: "I will come Sunday."

When Sunday came, his Mother urged him to go to church with them to West Farmington.

Charles L.: "No, I am going to the Hosner School House."

Mother: "Why go so far away, when you can ride all the way with us?"

Charles L.: "I want a change. They say that this minister at Hosner's School House is fine. He is entertaining."

Mother: "There must be some other reason. You wouldn't ride that far just to hear a Methodist preacher."

Charles L.: "Henry Forbush is home after his trip to California. I want to see him." (and he might have added "Louisa".)

II

Charles went regularly to the Hosner Church services for some months and on the first trip he

MICHIGAN TRAILMAKERS 93

and Henry talked over the prospects of farming compared to business enterprises.

Charles L.: "Do you think farming has as great a future for us young men born and bred on the farm?"

Henry: "I surely do or I would not have invested in the farm in Pleasant Valley. Your farms in Oakland County are not far from good markets and you have some improved roads. There are the Pontiac and Detroit, and the Pontiac, Walled Lake and Ann Arbor highways which are not far from us. The Detroit & Pontiac railroad runs through Birmingham, only eight miles from us. Have you seen the little wood heated engine? The farmer who is near the track and can furnish dry wood for the engine has a good job. The road uses lots of ties over which they place long wooden rails sawed out, on top of which long strips of strap iron, called "snake heads" are nailed to carry the wheels of the engine and cars. This railroad gives us eastern markets by way of Detroit and the Great Lakes. The Detroit and St. Joseph Railroad (Michigan Central) is in operation between Ann Arbor and Detroit. The passenger coaches are large omnibusses on frames and it has freight cars also. This county is building plank roads. There is the Detroit and Grand River Turnpike running through Farmington, Novi, Howell and Lansing, part of which is planked. This gives us easy access by way of Farmington to the best market in the state—Detroit. There will soon be a plank road from Pontiac through Birmingham and Royal Oak to Detroit."

94   MICHIGAN TRAILMAKERS

Charles L.: "There is talk in the Free Press and the Pontiac Gazette of establishing a College of Agriculture in the state. The college ought to help us farmers materially."

Henry: "Yes, the college will help us all to farm more intelligently and consequently we can raise more wheat, corn and oats and potatoes to the acre. Then, too, the cities are growing rapidly and factories are opening up everywhere; the country is prosperous, a survey is being made for a Pacific Railway connecting the east with the west. There will be a ready sale with good prices for all we can raise. New machinery, such as mowers, reapers, threshers, will increase the acreage and crop production. Another important aid to farmers is the importation of well bred cattle, the Durhams, the Holsteins, and the Clydesdale and Percheron horses, and the Hampshire and Shropshire sheep. Stock raising is a coming business. Stock farmers are going away down to Texas for steers and are bringing them to Illinois and Michigan to be fed for the market. The farmers are organizing in clubs and associations for social purposes as well as for information."

Charles L.: "Will politics have any effect on our farming? The slavery question looms on the horizon. The Missouri Compromise didn't settle it. The Kansas-Nebraska Bill is causing bloodshed. There was a mass meeting in Detroit to protest to Congress against the passage of the bill. Zach Chandler spoke against the bill; Lewis Cass spoke in its behalf. The Republican party made up of Democrats,

Whigs, and Free Soilers, who opposed the extension of slavery, met in Jackson, July 6, 1854, and organized and pledged itself to work for the repeal of this Kansas-Nebraska bill. Haven't you heard about that homely but honest man Abe Lincoln of Illinois, a Whig, who is becoming the champion of anti-slavery, and Stephen Douglas—Senator Douglas of Washington—the champion of slavery? I'm afraid we will have war."

Henry: "If we do have war, many of us young men will have to go. We will need all the rest to raise enough produce to care for the army and for the non-agricultural workers. I still think we will do well to stick to our farms. Look about us. You see good barns and houses on most farms, and they are well stocked with cattle, horses, sheep and hogs. The farmers are prosperous and are making money. Isn't this true of your father?"

III

After living in the Bachelor neighborhood for more than twenty years, and clearing and developing a good farm with barns, sheds and corncribs, Edwin sold the farm and bought another—the Dandison farm—north of the east end of the Middle Straits Lake. The next year found him settled permanently on a 160-acre farm south of the Middle Straits, formerly owned by William Green. Frank Orr also left the old neighborhood soon after the Forbushes settled on their new farm, and settled on another farm on the north side of the Pontiac and Ann Arbor road, still in West Bloomfield. Charles L. discovered good fishing in the Middle Straits and on Saturday afternoons he would go there ostensibly to fish.

Chalk said to him: "There is good fishing in Walled Lake, only three miles away. Why walk five miles to the Straits? Do you catch bigger and better fish?"

Charles L: "I certainly do, the lake is full of large roach, sunfish, perch, rock bass, and pickerel. They ain't all fished out over there like they are at Walled Lake."

He soon began to stay all night and the following Sunday.

Cordon said: "Louisa, things look kind of serious between you and Charles." She: "No! he doesn't care for me. He would rather fish. He is lonesome and comes to see you and Pa and to talk over raising hogs and corn." But she couldn't help being interested in him, although she was bashful, shy, retiring, and would seldom look into his gray eyes, wistful with love. Why shouldn't she be interested in this fine looking young man, stout, robust, muscular, with a high forehead, covered with coal black hair, with a cowlick in the center where the part should come? He was five feet, nine inches tall, stood erect, six inches taller than she was. Besides he was interested in the preaching meetings, so was she.

His mother couldn't understand why Charles L. had taken to fishing every Saturday and to remaining at the Forbushes over Sunday and to going to church every Sunday with Eddie, Louisa, and Lavancha. Soon he found excuses for riding his best horse to the Straits on mid-week evenings. Finally one soft, balmy May evening, the bright full moon, high up overhead with no visible support with fleecy clouds passing over her face, shone through the thick foliage of a stately sugar maple and cast her tender rays of light upon Charles and Louisa sitting on the grassy bank of the lake across the road from the house. The bull frogs down by the water were singing their basso profundo and the little frogs were croaking in mere happiness to be alive and to have a home in the rushes; a tree toad on the first limb of the maple tree was calling for rain, an owl in a nearby tree looked down and purred "To whit! to woo!; and a bird in the forest across the lake was calling to his mate "Whip Poor Will", "Whip Poor Will" and a lonely hen loon floating on the waters of the west end of the lake near the Richardsons was intermittently calling across the lake for her mate. It was a poetic evening in the mating season. Charles gently slipped his arm around Louisa's waist and pressed her to him. There was a sympathetic understanding in their eyes which shone with a new brightness. Their lips touched! New ideals and purposes were created, a new home was established. Their lives immediately began the process of being knitted together with common ideals, common purposes.

On the twelfth day of June 1856, they were married by Reverend Samuel Morse, pastor of the Baptist Church at Walled Lake, in the early afternoon, in the shade of that beautiful old maple tree which spread out his branches loaded with green leaves to protect the bridal couple from the hot rays of the sun. The bride wore a two piece black silk dress. The waist was tight fitting, sleeves full and flowing. The skirt was tight about the waist but full and flowing at the bottom. Aunt Hannah placed some red rose buds in her knot of black hair, and a bouquet of them in full bloom on her left breast. Charles looked fine in his high heeled boots, his Prince Albert coat which Louisa later called his "Alpaca wedding coat." If you could have seen them standing side by side under the spreading maple with spots of sunlight filtering through the leaves and falling upon their figures, you would have said, "A fine couple, a good match". Charles was erect, towering above her six inches, black hair with a cowlick in front, giving the effect of a pompadour, and was dressed in his long black coat and vest with white collar and a black bow tie, and black pantaloons to match. She looked beautiful in her black silk, with the red roses on her breast and in her hair. The red of the roses blended with the black hair and the black silk to produce a beautiful brunette.

CHAPTER IX

ISAAC LAMB AND HIS KNITTING MACHINE

Charles L.: "How do you like the looks of this house, Louisa? Not much like the log houses you have lived in, is it?"

Louisa: "No, I won't know how to act in that big house."

Charles L.: "Let's go inside." (They enter the front door under a porch). "Here is a large room you can use for the dinner table—an ample room for a large family."

Louisa: "What's in here? (pushing the door open to her left). Why, this is the room the Smith's used for a parlor."

They wandered through into the kitchen, pantry, woodshed, and then into the several rooms upstairs. Then they looked out to the east and saw the horse barn, the walls of which were built up, the first story out of cobble stones; to the north of this was the hay barn, cattle sheds, poultry house and smoke house, and over in the barn yard was last year's straw stack. This was the Eldad Smith farm in West Bloomfield about a mile north of Charles Severance's homestead. The Smiths and Severances had been neighbors. Eldad settled here in 1828 on a 200-acres of timberland. During his thirty years residence, he cleared his farm, leaving an ample wood lot, dug up the "hard heads" and piled them in heaps in various parts of the field, fenced his farm and with cross section zigzag rail fences, divided it into lots —meadow lots, pasture lots, and lots for corn, oats, wheat, and the like. He erected a large frame house, nearly as large but older than Charles's big white house. He added barns, corn cribs, hay lofts, and other improvements so that when Charles contracted for the purchase of it for Charles L. and Chalkley it was an up-to-date farm, comparatively speaking.

Charles L. put in his savings to which it was said his father added a considerable amount. In fact, it is said that he mortgaged his farm to raise the money to make the first payment. Chalkley, unmarried, added his mite. Charles L. moved in as manager, furnished the house, provided a home for Chalkley and bed and board for one or two hired men. Horses and wagons, plows, cultivators, mower, reaper, cows, hogs, sheep were purchased and secured by chattel mortgages. Seed corn, seed wheat, seed potatoes were borrowed from Charles or Edwin or purchased on time. On Sunday afternoon in the late spring, Charles L. and Louisa went down the lane to the far pasture to salt the sheep and the cattle, and passed by the twenty-acre lot of oats.

Charles L.: "Look there! See that field of oats, see that dark green color and see how the plants cover the ground? If nothing happens, there will be a bumper crop. Look at the corn on the other side. Believe its good for hundred bushel of ears to the acre. This is a good farm. The potatoes are pushing out of the ground. Let's pray for a good season so we can pay off the mortgages on our stock and tools."

Louisa: "Is that the Andrews farm off to the southeast?"

"Yes", replied Charles L. "Your folk live north about three miles and Cousin Frank is over north on the Pontiac road about three miles away. To the west of us in that little frame house lives Seymour Deveraux who settled soon after Eldad and assisted at the raising of Pa's log house. Zeke Dye is still farther west. I do believe that cousin Van is much interested in his daughter. Pa's house is just across the marsh to the south, near enough so we can go there often and can borrow his tools until we get some of our own."

Louisa: "We can't have a better place to live and raise our family, with neighbors and our own folk near by. What shall I do with all this work when Perry arrives? Maybe sister Lavancha can come and help a few weeks."

They talked over many plans for the future and built any number of air castles and were happy. In the fall Perry came to gladden their hearts and the panic to sadden them.

There had been large amounts of money spent on railroad construction without any returns on the investment. The Michigan Southern was extended from Monroe to Chicago in 1852 and the Michigan Central was completed in the same year as far west as Chicago; the Chicago and Rock Island construction reached Rock Island in 1854. There was an over speculation in stocks and in lands in Illinois, Wisconsin, and other middlewestern states. As in 1837, land companies purchased acreages with payment of less than five per cent of their normal worth. The banks again suspended specie payment, money couldn't be had on any kind of security. Fortunately for Charles L. and Chalkley, their borrowed money came from friends and relatives and unfortunately their wonderful crops couldn't be sold because the jobbers couldn't get money to ship the produce. Many families lost heavily but the losses throughout Michigan were not so heavy as in the "Wild Cat" bank era of 1837.

In the spring of 1858, Isaac W. Lamb a youth of nineteen years visited his cousins, Charles L. and Chalkley. He was the son of a Baptist preacher, Roswell Lamb, pastor of a church in the little town of Hartland, north of Milford. Roswell and Caleb Lamb came in 1824 to Michigan with their father, Nehemiah, who was sent by the N. Y. Baptist Convention as a missionary to the pioneers of Oakland County. Reverend Nehemiah and Reverend Caleb were pastors at Farmington and Walled Lake and other villages in Michigan for many years. Caleb took to Homeopathic medical practice for a few years. Due to his practice his sister Martha kept a supply of homeopathic pills in the house for immediate use in case one of the children should be sick. Charles L. learned the curative properties of aconite, belladonna, pulsatella, mercury sol, and the like, so that he could dose the children whenever they needed medical attention. Less is known about

Roswell but he was like his father and brother Caleb, one of the substantial men and loyal preachers of the Baptist faith. Isaac born in Salem, near Northville, was also a preacher but was more than a preacher. He was an inventive genius. He built a machine for braiding whip lashes out of four strands at first, then out of any number of strands later.

At the time of his visit he was trying to perfect his machine for knitting stockings. He went into details in explaining his invention to Charles L. and Chalkley. His machine, he claimed, was an assured success. He needed money for completing his invention and for getting it patented and then more money to make the parts and to begin the establishment of a knitting factory. "Here is a machine", he said, "which works perfectly. All we need is capital sufficient to get it patented and to begin the knitting business. It will pay big money. A few hundred invested now will yield thousands in a few years."

Charles L.: "Is it ready for the patent?"

Isaac: "Nearly, a few improvements need to be added."

Charles L.: "Can't you sell the patent to a firm or corporation?"

Isaac: "Yes, but I wouldn't get much. I want to form the company, then we will have all that's made. Profits should accrue to the inventor and to the stockholders."

Charles and Louisa talked the matter over. Louisa

said: "I don't know anything about inventions, you will have to decide. I am satisfied on this farm."

Charles L.: "Well, farming isn't what it used to be. This has been a hard winter, crops not too good, prices low."

Louisa: "Well, let us not go into an uncertainty. Eldad Smith made money off this place, why shouldn't we?"

Charles L.: "Why yes, but here is a chance to make a lot of money without having to work for it. Just think, as soon as the factory starts we will begin to get our money back. Everybody would wear these cheap (in price) stockings knitted by machinery. Then, too, it would be a question of getting our money out of this farm to invest if we should want to take stock in Cousin Isaac's invention."

Chalkley: "I will buy you out if you give me time in which to pay but I think you are foolish to sell and invest in that uncertainty."

Louisa: "I don't care for 'get rich quick schemes'. I don't understand it at all."

Charles L. was inexperienced in business. His father never gave his boys the responsibility of marketing produce and buying provisions, and buying stock. The boys did the work, the father kept the business transactions in his own hands. Charles L. knew nothing about inventions, the cost of perfecting a machine, securing a patent, establishing a factory for manufacturing the parts. Isaac knew but little about the way of doing things and the initial cost. It was all very wonderful to him.

Comparatively few inventors do have this information but these were minor matters compared to the results which they could see materializing in dreamland.

Charles L. sold the equity in his farm to his brother Chalkley, invested all he had, then gave promissory notes for additional shares. He then settled down as his brother Chalkley's hired man.

CHAPTER X

A NEW START

SAINT JOHNS

I

In 1864, six years after Charles L. invested in Isaac Lamb's knitting machine, one might have seen a pioneer with his little family and household goods driving west from the home of his boyhood. He and Louisa sat on the spring seat in front of the wagon drawn by a team of gray horses. Louisa held baby Palmer on her lap well wrapped, as this September morning was frosty and the air was crisp. Arthur and Eugene were here and there on the load of household goods, sometimes in front looking over the dashboard at the horses and sometimes romping on the feather ticks just back of the seat. Perry, the eldest boy was deceased. The top box wagon was really full. There were quilts and other kinds of bedding. There were dishes, tables, stoves, wash tubs, boiler, wash board, bedstead, cradle, clock, candle moulds, plow and drag, forks, hoes, and the like. In the bottom of the wagon box was the little trunk covered with pig skin with the hair on. This trunk was an heirloom purchased in New York by Louisa's grandmother Bachelor. In it was folded carefully and stowed away neatly

Louisa's wedding dress and Charles L.'s "alpaca coat" together with the blue and white coverlet which her Mother wove from the wool she cleaned and carded, and a few other precious articles hallowed by remembrances. Behind the wagon and tethered to the rod in the end board of the box was the young cow which her father gave Louisa to take to the new farm. They were off on their long journey at daylight. Charles and Martha and their two youngest—Jotham and Elmina—who were still at home, walked to the gate and a piece down the road, then waved a farewell and a Godspeed to them. As Charles and Martha returned to the house they both thought of the same event,—the trailmakers of 1835 who started from Geneva, New York, in the covered wagon drawn by oxen. Charles said: "History repeats itself. I hope they will have fewer hardships than we have had."

The pioneers stopped at the Eldad Smith place where they got their first auspicious start in life to say good-by to Chalkley and Martha and their children. They passed on in sadness and with keen regrets for their decision to sell out and buy stock in the knitting machine. Their route was the Pontiac and Ann Arbor Road past Frank Orr's where they stopped again to say good-by, then by way of Pontiac to Holly, Owosso and St. Johns where Charles had purchased a forty-acre farm for $500. St. Johns was a little town on the Clinton River named by Caleb Lamb. When the route of the Detroit and Milwaukee railway was surveyed in 1852, Caleb was the Baptist minister in Clinton County. He had helped survey the plat of the city carrying one end of the chain. He cleared some land and set out fruit trees. A stock company was formed which purchased the land where the town was to be built. Families had already settled here before the survey for the railroad was made and before the town was named. Several names were proposed, such as Rich-Mond, Sweglesville, Johnsville. Caleb said call it "St. Johns." Swegle said, "For some reasons, I would be in favor of St. Johns". Caleb replied: "Amen! St. Johns, let it be." "And thus the child was christened and thus the name remains to this day."

Charles L. and family settled in a good neighborbod five miles south and one mile west of St. Johns. His brother, John and family, were already there, so was his sister Adelia who married Glover Williams, so when the pioneers arrived on the second day out, they were welcomed into the homes of John and of Adelia and were feasted for several days before they settled in the snug little house on their new farm. It was a beautiful forty-acre farm, covered largely with hardwood trees, lying level, easy to work, good soil, sandy loam, well mixed with clay which bore good crops. They were happy to have a farm of their own after Charles had worked as a hired man for his brother Chalkley, his father and Louisa's father. He settled here during the progress of the Civil War which was a prosperous time for farmers. All the farmers not in the army were needed to produce enough wheat, oats, corn, hay, beef and pork for the army and navy and for the city dwellers. Farm machinery was high but the reaper made it possible for a farmer to raise much more wheat with the same labor which he employed before the war.

Farm machinery was so high that only a few farmers could own it. The reaper, which made it possible for the farmers to raise larger acreages of wheat and oats with the same labor which he employed before the war, cut the grain for the neighborhood. There was much exchange of work in this community. Harvesting and haying required more hands than one farm could support so we find in Charles's record that he exchanged work on jobs which required more than one man. His oxen and plow broke ground for his neighbor at $2.00 a day. When he couldn't pay in kind he paid or received as the case might be, a dollar a day and board for common labor such as hoeing corn; a dollar and a half a day for haying; and two dollars a day for harvest work. The farmer who kept a hired man paid on an average of $18.00 a month.

The prices of farm products during these years remained on the whole, at a high level which justified this labor wage. It has been pointed out that "the year 1867 was one of market prosperity. Wheat was quoted in St. Paul at $1.40 a bushel" although there was a fall in the prices of corn and oats.

After demobilization at the close of the war, many soldiers were employed in industrial plants; others went back to the farms and became producers. This was a period of very great industrial activity in the north. The great cattle ranches in Texas and the southwest began to supply the incipient packing houses of Armour, Morris and Swift. The development of the Pennsylvania oil fields, and the building of railroads to the west of the Mississippi and to the coast which furnished employment for a vast number of laborers, thousands of whom were immigrants from Europe. The Union Pacific, Chicago and Northwestern, the Chicago and Rock Island, Chicago, Burlington and Quincy opened up the prairies between the Mississippi River and the Rocky mountains for settlement. The tide of immigration set in and pushed the border of civilization to the mountains. Many farmers living in the middle west pulled up stakes and went west to settle; soldiers went west. Scandinavians entered the United States and moved northwest and settled in Minnesota and the Dakotas.

Charles L., in whom the pioneer spirit still survived, felt strongly the urge to go west. The urge became intensified by the tempting offer of an eighty-acre farm for $1,000 twelve miles west of Rock Island. His brother's wife's sister, Mrs. Harry Conley owned the farm and while on a visit to Michigan enthused her relatives with the great opportunities for farmers in the west. Thousands of farmers took the trail. Many of them had little to take besides themselves and oxen or horses and wagons, very few tools to work with. Charles L. sold his St. Johns farm for a favorable sum, $450 above the purchase price, and without seeing the Illinois farm, contracted for the purchase of it in December, 1866.

Early in April 1865 when Charles L. was plowing ground for his corn crop, little Arthur ran down to the field shouting to him, "Lincoln's shot! Lincoln's shot!" His father stopped the horses, "How do you know?" "A farmer rode by on horseback while I was sitting on the gate post in front of the house and shouted, 'Lincoln's shot, tell your Pa', and galloped on up the road toward Uncle Johns'. I slid off the post, ran to the house, told Ma, and now I am here to tell you. Pa, who is Lincoln?" Lincoln's name was a household word in this little village of St. Johns and in the rural homes. Families had followed in the newspapers, the course and events of the War and of the leading men in Washington and the commanding generals. This family developed a love for Lincoln and Grant. In fact, Charles L. in later years had a lithograph of Grant, his wife and four boys hanging on the walls of his living room. They felt a personal loss in Lincoln's tragic death.

John, Charles, and Glover quit work, drove to the village for more news. Then they found that Lincoln had been foully murdered by a shot from the revolver of Wilkes Booth, April 11, 1865. The whole country was shocked at the news of this tragedy but no town was more shocked and distressed than this little village of St. Johns. The people in this rural community in Central Michigan loved him and were indignant at the foul treatment of the assassin.

II

During the eight or nine years since Charles invested in Isaac's invention of the knitting machine, Isaac had perfected the machine, secured a patent,

September 15, 1863, and after several unsuccessful attempts to organize a corporation for the manufacture of the machines, the Lamb Knitting Machine Company was organized in Springfield, Massachusetts, and a second one in Rochester, New York, 1865. Both of these were consolidated in 1867 and a factory opened in Chiopee Falls, Massachusetts. A small knitting factory was opened at Northville. His machine was patented in England, Belgium and France and received a silver medal at the Paris Exposition in 1867. Thousands of dollars were made out of the Lamb knitting factories but the inventor Isaac received only a few thousand. He went back to his ministry and served the little Baptist church at Novi Corners.

Neither was he so badly off as Charles L. who lost all the money invested in the original company and was left stranded with promissory notes in favor of Issac yet to be paid. He made a new start in business when he purchased the forty-acre farm near St. Johns but the "dunning" letters from Isaac were a constant aggravation. Charles L. reasoned with himself, "Why should I 'drop' a few hundred dollars more into this business which will never yield any returns on the stock?" and besides he needed all he could earn to care for his growing family. The letters continued to come to Charles for sixteen years when an attorney in Andalusia where Charles was then living called to collect. He handed Charles the note, he took it, looked at it carefully then tore off his signature and handed it back to the attorney, who had a sudden attack of violent anger. Charles was ignorant of the statute of limitations which relieved him from payment and of the liability of imprisonment for the act of tearing off his signature. Consequently, another note was given and paid a few dollars at a time out of the earnings of his eldest son who peddled meat to earn money to support the family.

CHAPTER XI
THE ILLINOIS FARM

"Every hope has a rendezvous with disappointment"

I

The sun rose silently and pleasantly one April morning in 1867 and scattered the fog which had settled down upon the Mississippi River and Andalusia Creek. After the showers of the night before, the farms on the south bluff of the River as far as one could see were steaming. The trees and bushes in the nearby woods and along the creeks and rivers lifted their dark, wet branches to the sun for a drying. A little house and an old barn washed clean the night before looked black and hideous, but welcome, as they came into sight with the gradual lifting of the fog which had completely enveloped everything. Charles and Louisa and the children—Arthur, Eugene, Palmer, and Henry, in his Mother's arms, were out early to get their bearing and "to see what there was to see." To the north of them was a well cultivated farm with a good two story farm house and a large barn with cows and horses in the barnyard; to the east on the opposite side of the highway appeared to be the roof of a house but advancing closer to the road they saw a good house in the little hollow twenty rods from the road—a

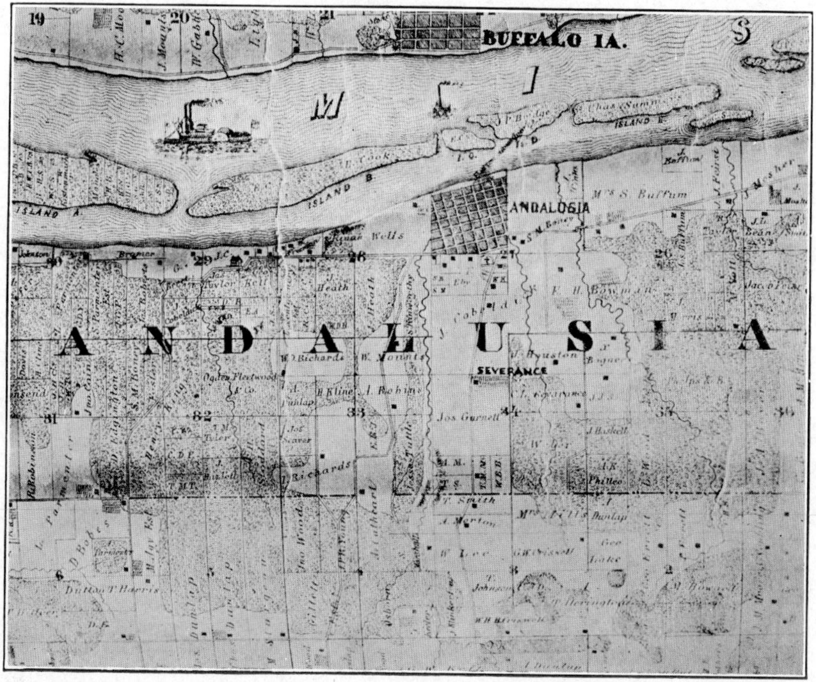
BUFFALO IA.
ANDALOSIA
ANDALUSIA
SEVERANCE
ISLAND A
ISLAND B
ISLAND E

house set well into the ground and banked up with dirt to keep the cold out in the winter. There was a good barn and a large straw stack in the barnyard, and two boys and their dad milking cows, feeding pigs, teaching calves to drink. When Charles mentioned the boys in the barnyard, Eugene and Parm who couldn't see, cried, "We want to see, too", and climbed to the top of the rail fence. Then off to the west, were the woods in the valley and on the banks and adjoining acres of the Andalusia creek which rises way down south and flowed through an avenue of forest trees and loses its waters in the great Mississippi.

The birds gave them a cordial welcome. The robins hopped about on the grass; the sparrows sailed overhead and lit on the roof of the house, and in the branches of the big tree nearby; the blackbirds came to investigate and to hope that the new farmer would plant some garden corn and raise some raspberries. The bobwhite from a distant field, keeping his flock out of sight of the boys, called to them, "Bob White! Bob-bob-white!" and the old crows sailed over to size up the farmer and called in joyful caws to their mates in the woods down by the creek, "the farmer will plant corn", "the farmer will plant corn", "cawn", "cawn", "cawn".

Then they examined the barn with a lean-to shed and the little weatherbeaten frame house of three rooms and an attic. The house looked comfortable to Louisa who had lived in log houses until she was married. To Charles the house was a small matter, at any rate they were content to be pioneers in this

Black Hawk country. Charles said: "I will build a lean-to on the west side of the house for sleeping rooms and I will make a bigger barn. My first straw stack will provide a warm room in its base for cows and sheep. I will dig a well near the house and plant an orchard on the lot north of the house. I must clear more land and break it up for crops. What more could we expect for a thousand dollars in war time than this farm with thirty acres under cultivation and a house to live in—eighty acres—only three miles from the village of Andalusia and nine miles from Rock Island—a good market. We ought to make a living off this farm and add improvements after we reap our first harvest."

Then they looked about the farm which had been purchased unseen. The soil was a clay loam in a subsoil of reddish brown clay which cropped out on the erosions of the creek bank and the gulley. Andalusia Creek cut through the west end of the farm and dropped through the bluffs into the valley on the north in a cut some fifty or sixty feet deep. Directly north of the house was the head of a ravine which widened and deepened as it cut through the edge of the bluff back of John Houston's buildings. The remainder of the farm was comparatively level of which thirty acres had been cultivated; the remainder supported prairie grass, shrubs, brush and trees. The virgin soil was fertile, the other fairly so.

On their trip from Pontiac to Chicago and to Rock Island, members of the family brought a few articles with them and had the pigskin covered trunk checked to its destination. Charles, of course, carried the heaviest baggage; Arthur carried a roll tied up and held in place with a stout cord, Eugene carried a few children's clothes in a small box, Louisa carried baby Henry and shawls and wraps for him and for herself. Louisa was desperately sick on the lake trip from New Haven to Chicago owing to rough weather. Charles was reminded of the pioneer trip of his parents across Lake Erie from Buffalo to Detroit on their way to the Michigan forests when they encountered high seas. If he could be as successful in his prairie adventure as they were in acquiring and developing homes in Michigan, he would be satisfied. There was a long tedious wait in the Chicago station as the Chicago and Rock Island railroad was new; the passenger traffic was light which necessitated few trains. During the wait Arthur and Eugene looked around in the station and discovered other boys. They had bundles wrapped in bandanna handkerchiefs. The men and women looked dirty and shabby, wore shawls around their shoulders and had beside them great bundles tied up in sheets and blankets. They talked in a language which Arthur and Eugene did not understand. They talked with their hands, their heads, and their lips. They gesticulated while Arthur and Eugene stood with wide open eyes and mouths and watched them. There were two types of boys, one with black coarse hair, dark skin, bright, black sparkling eyes, red bandanna kerchiefs about their necks—Italians; the other, stolid, heavy set, rather ponderous, light colored, heavy hair, strong physique, strong characters, with determination showing in every feature and expression of the face, long jeans and large felt hats—German.

Arthur edged around to his father and said: "Who are they, Pa, and where are they going?"

Charles: "Immigrants going west and south to take up land."

Arthur: "What are immigrants, Pa?"

Charles: "Families who come across the ocean from Germany and Italy and from other countries to make their homes in Michigan, Illinois and other states."

Eugene whispered to his Mother: "I'm afraid of them. I hope they don't settle near us."

II

Eugene, the second son, who was nearly five years of age when the family settled on this new farm and thirteen years when Charles sold out and returned to Michigan, and who after attaining his majority, secured a college education through his own efforts, has recalled the life on this farm and written the record from which the writer quotes:

"That first year was a hectic year. Father knew that he must have good full crops to pay interest on the mortgages on his farm and on his chattels and to pay his groceries. Mother was ill much of the time, barely able to feed the family. At early dawn Father was out to feed his horses, to milk the cows, to 'slop' the pigs and cut firewood for the day. He was in the fields with the plow before seven. He would come in at night and tell Mother he had plowed two acres or two and a half acres. After supper he would go into the field and dig up roots or dig out stones as long as he could see. When the ground was ready for corn planting, he took his hoe and corn with a few pumpkin seeds mixed in, which he put into a little sack fastened on in front of him by long strings tied behind his back. He dug the holes with the hoe in the right hand and dropped four kernels into the hill with his left. He planted from daylight to dark, then for weeks Arthur and I had to watch the crows and the squirrels to keep them from digging up the corn. Then came the severe task of planting potatoes after the ground was ready. He took a grain bag, tied one corner of the bottom and one of the top together, filled the sack with a peck or more of potatoes cut up so that at least one eye was in a piece, threw the sack over the shoulder then started down the row dropping three pieces in a hill. We followed covering them with our hoes and sometimes took our turn at dropping potatoes. After planting time, he hired a two-ox team and plowed new ground from which the brush and trees had been removed. He found it to his advantage to hire a man to work on the farm while he worked in the harvest field for his neighbors at $2.00 a day. When he asked a farmer on the prairie for a job in the harvest field, the farmer looked him over! "You're too thin for man's work behind the reaper," but Father bound his beat—one-third the reaper cut—without difficulty. He knew how to do it from his long experience, his muscles were like steel and he carried no excess weight. As a young man he weighed 175 to 180 pounds but now with worry and hard work he was reduced to about 140 pounds. After the fall wheat sowing and the cutting and shocking and husking the corn was over, Father began clearing the woodland, splitting the oak logs into rails for fences, trimming the limbs for firewood and cutting the maple and beech and other timber in four feet lengths and selling it at $4.00 a cord in Rock Island in the winter while the sleighing was good. The next year was a repetition of the first. Up early, to bed late. The farm showed the improvements due to Father's tireless efforts in tilling the soil and cultivating the crops, which resulted in the improvements around the house and barn, and the ten-acre apple orchard north of the house.

"But the year 1868 was disastrous for the farmers on the plains because of over production. Vast acreages on the prairies had been subdued by the plow share and such quantities of wheat and corn were produced that the market was glutted. Wheat and other grains were piled up in the shipping centers of the west and besides there was a heavy falling off in the consumption of headstuffs in the eastern and in the foreign markets. Wheat was quoted in St. Paul in 1867 at $1.40 a bushel; in 1865 at 95c; and in 1869 at 75c.

"The following year, 1869, Father concluded that he could make more money at masonry than he could working the farm. He therefore combined the two. He hired Mr. Erret to break up new land and paid mostly in trade selling mutton at 16 2/3c a pound, four-foot wood at $3.00 a cord, a cow at $40.00, a calf at $5.00, but Erret was evidently not a careful man. He partially ruined one of the horses by overheating it in his attempt to plow as much as possible. He was paid $4.00 an acre for his plowing. The more acres the more money. Father assessed the damage at $25.00 whereupon he quit. Father hired out to lay stone at 75c a perch and board but preferred to work by the job, for when he worked overtime or hurried on the job he would get pay for the hurry and the longer hours. He dug a cistern and plastered the sides with cement for $15.00, laid an underpinning wall under the school house, in the village for $18.50, which is there in good condition fifty years later, dug a well for Mr. Houston and lathed and plastered a house for $33.50. With the help of a hired man, who was not interested in how much he could do, he kept the farm going. He continued this arrangement for several years receiving $2.50 a day for his mason work and paying $15.00 a month and board for a hired man or boy.

"Our neighbors, the Houstons, to the north of us whose farm joined ours, were past middle life. Mr. Houston had used his strength and energy in making his eighty acres pay for itself. He was taking life rather moderately now. He was slow to anger, considerate, not careful to keep his stock within his own fences. Father's corn and potato fields were adjacent to his pasture lot one spring, in which was an old sow with a litter of young pigs. Rail fences are seldom proof against pigs and chickens. These pigs were old enough to root for corn and potatoes in the hills. Father had already replanted several rows next to Houston's and told him the damage the pigs were doing. One morning when he started to the field to work he saw the pigs rooting up his corn. He rushed into the field with rapid strides, his anger rising with every step. He caught a Poland China youngster which missed the hole in the fence and struck it on the forehead with his right fist. The pig straightened out, then relaxed with trembling feet and died.

"The Strohmeiers who lived in the house in the valley across the road were Germans. Bill and Gus were older than Arthur and myself. We hadn't settled in our home before Bill and Gus came up to the road, got astride the rail fence, and looked us over. The Strohmeiers came from Germany and settled here several years earlier than we and had made a good beginning. They were different in their thinking, in their living. They lived apart, there were no other Germans in the neighborhood. Mr. Strohmeier was a stolid man, of large physique, of enormous energy and wonderful endurance. The boys were good fellows and playmates much of the time when we had time to play. It was my great surprise to see the family at dinner eating clabbered milk with teaspoons as we eat custard. We went to the village school together, sometimes the boys would come to our house on Sundays to play with us. Mother was very particular about the way we spent Sunday. Often when she was ill we would go to the swimming hole in Andalusia Creek in our back lot. One warm Sunday afternoon when Bill and Gus and Arthur and I were enjoying a good swim, mother arrived on the scene with a good switch in her hand. We didn't have time to put our clothes on before she caught us and marched us to the house. We boys got on better together than our fathers did. Strohmeier's corn patch was just across the road from our house. It was in full tassels and silk. Our chickens loved to hunt bugs in this cornfield. When Strohmeier saw them he raged with madness. Father had just driven them out of the corn patch one afternoon when Mr. Strohmeier and the boys rushed through the corn with pitchforks in their hands with which to do him bodily damage, then stopped at the fence, damned him, shook their fists at him and promised to fork him if he got into their cornfield again, but father walked quietly into our house and said nothing.

"The Goodes lived farther south. We were not on intimate terms with them. The old man was profane, his vocabulary was made up largely of cuss words. He used them on his boys who were now young men. He was a vigorous athletic man, capable of strenuous work. The Goodes always put up ice in the winter for summer use. One winter when they were cutting and hauling ice from the river by the village, the old man accidentally slipped and fell into the opening, but caught and supported himself from sinking by keeping his hands on the ice. His eldest son reached over caught him by the hair of the head and pushed him under the water and then pulled him up and swore at him. "Damn you", he said, "unless you promise to be good and treat us decent I will shove you under the ice." He promised and begged for mercy. He was pulled out, wrapped in blankets and taken home about three miles away on a cold winter day.

We reached the Templeton's by going to the back end of our farm and across Andalusia Creek on a log and up the farther bank and beyond. When mother was ill, Mrs. Templeton was the first to come to our assistance. Our cordial relations added zest to life. Then, too, Cad Templeton, the daughter, about Arthur's age, was a typical girl of the rural districts, and especially charming and attractive to us youngsters. Coming up the creek bottom from the village school, I was once caught in a terrible thunderstorm and was drenched and scared and nearly exhausted when Father appeared. He wrapped his coat around me and hugged me to him and ran into the Templeton's house where we received warm welcome and solicitous attention. The Houstons were good neighbors, too. Mrs. Houston was a friend in need often when Mother was sick.

"Mother's enjoyment, if she could be said to have had any pleasure under conditions of ill health and strain of over-work and responsibility, was the inspiration and fellowship of the church service and in her family when she gathered the children around her for evening prayer. The Baptist church in the village was a small frame church, rectangular in form, the door in one end; the pulpit and choir loft on a raised platform in the other. The aisle was through the middle; the straight back benches on either side. Here the family sat through the morning service, joining in the singing of the hymns and enjoying the Sunday School after the Church service. It was a real joy to worship in this little church and open their hearts to the soothing and refreshing influences of this hour of worship. The little chats with the women of the church in which Mother confided her troubles gave relief to her burdened mind. Then they went back up that steep clay hill, the horses pulling the wagon at a snail's pace, to begin their Monday's work with renewed interest and vigor.

"When Mother couldn't go on account of the muddy roads or the heavy snow, she sent us on foot down the creek bottom. When we returned, in summer, we stopped at the swimming hole to cool off, or in Dr. Bowman's strawberry patch or in his grape arbor, or in Houston's orchard to satisfy a nagging of the stomach.

"Mother's religious faith was the steadying force of her life. She cared little for money, but she held fast to spiritual realities. In her own illness and in that of the children and later of Father, she was buoyed up by her firm and abiding faith which comforted her and gave her reassurance that everything is for the best and that nothing is so bad that it might not be worse.

"The Sabbath was a day for church and Sunday School and following these services a day for rest. There were no games; no swimming. Father would walk over the farm to see the corn grow, the wheat heads fill, to salt the cows and the sheep and to estimate the melon crop on the creek bottom. The soil here was fertile; the melons large and delicious. The boys of the village frequently visited the melon patch at moonlight when the melons were at their best.

"Father and I were watching the patch one moonlight night from a hiding in the bushes on the bluffs. Father pulled the trigger of his shot gun when we discovered a lot of men and boys in the patch with five sacks already filled. The men caught the sacks by the bottom and spilling the melons on the ground as they ran like wild animals down the creek.

III

"Father was not a hard task master. He was indulgent. On a farm where there is only one man to do the work with the difficulty of finding an extra man occasionally, even if there had been money to pay him, the growing boys found their fill of work. Gus and Bill did hard, strenuous work. Arthur and I felt the urge to help, so in the course of years, we accomplished wonders for little boys. We helped Mother with the dishes, kept the wood box full, carried the water for the house up from the spring, a fourth of a mile away, drove the team on the drag. I rode the horse between the corn rows while Arthur handled the three-legged 'grasshopper' cultivator, brought the cows home from the woods at night, drove them to the spring to water in the cold winter when we had to cut holes in the ice so they could drink, and helped Father dig wells by manipulating the windlass above the mouth of the well by which one bucket of dirt was brought up and emptied while another was lowered to be filled, set up oat and wheat bundles, husked corn and helped load and stack the bundles and stalks, and a hundred other operations which boys from ten to fourteen might do.

"We had good times with work, with school and with play. The one big event of these years was Barnum's Circus in Rock Island, in the summer of 1871. We had seen posters in the village showing the elephants, camels, horseback riders, the clowns and the like. All the boys and men were talking about it. Everybody was going. Father hitched the horses to the wagon and started with the whole family early on circus day. We were there to see the wonderful parade. It was the 'greatest circus' on earth, live elephants taught to do things, horse races, chariot races, trapeze performances in mid-air, wild animals behind bars in specially constructed wagons, the loud roaring lion, the panther, the polar bear, the apes and monkeys, the striped horses, the trained dogs, and above all the funny clowns—the dear old clowns were never forgotten. We could think or talk of nothing else for days. We relived that circus day many, many times. Then, too, we were impressed with the big river about a mile wide, gliding smoothly, rhythmically, quietly by, carrying on its bosom, the row boats, the trunks of trees, boxes, boards—everything that floats on the water, silently down stream. In the dead of winter horses and sleighs and cutters might be seen going to and fro across the river and up and back to Rock

Island. We had no conception of the beginning of the river of water nor of its ending.

"The further fact that the Great Black Hawk Indian Chief and his tribes lived in this region and rowed back and forth across the river in their little canoes excited our wonder and admiration. The Black Hawk War in which Abraham Lincoln was a captain was waged for the possession of Rock Island, the river bottoms and adjacent territory in Illinois which had been ceded by the tribe to the United States. Black Hawk and his tribe were given lands across the river in Iowa in place of these holdings in Illinois."

IV

Life is complex. Many conditions and considerations enter into one's life. Hard and strenuous work over a period of years presupposed a good physique to begin with, with proper food, sleep and relaxation to keep the body in the best physical condition. A farmer needs his machine kept oiled and in repair so that it will produce results in crops, in livestock, in good buildings and the like, but he needs more, he needs business ability. It required one talent to produce a crop of wheat, another talent to market it to the best advantage. The farmers' big problem of the present day is not one of producing, but one of marketing. Charles showed a lack of business acumen when he sold out his equity in the Eldad Smith farm to his brother and invested in Lamb's knitting invention and again when he sold the St. John's farm and moved to the bluffs of the

Mississippi. He was never strong on making bargains for his own interests. He succeeded with great odds against him in developing his farm, putting practically all of it under cultivation, of raising a fine apple orchard, just ready to bear when he left it, of enlarging the house and barns and enclosing the whole farm with fences. It was well stocked and equipped with machinery when he sold out.

There were two things he did not reckon on while he was bending every energy and using every ounce of his vitality to make a living and pay for his farm —accidents and disease. It is said that a man doesn't appreciate his health until he loses it.

"Father went for the cows very early one morning. They had strayed away to a common wood where other cows pastured. He came upon a young brindle cow, mothering a young calf, wild with fear that something would get her baby calf. When she saw Father she rushed at him with head down. He grabbed the ends of her horns one in each hand. The impact of the horns on his breast was so great that it bruised him, knocked him over. The tight grasp of his hands over the ends of the sharp horns is all that saved his life. The cow rushed back to her calf, he rushed in the opposite direction over a fence. He suffered a hemorrhage then and serious trouble in later years."

"In the afternoon of March 17, 1871, when the stork was expected to bring Clara, a baby girl, into the home, Arthur and I were at the Strohmeier's helping the boys draw manure from the barnyard into the field near our house. After unloading we all got on the wagon, the horses became frightened and ran away, Arthur dropped between the loose boards to the ground with sand in his eyes and ears, manure on his face and clothes. He was unconscious when taken into the house. A hurry up trip to the village brought Dr. Bowman who examined him, washed the sand out of his eyes and cleaned him up. Fortunately he was not badly hurt. But Mother was badly scared. The Doctor stayed all night and presented us a baby sister next morning. Mother was sick much of the time during the eight years on the farm. This meant more work for Father, and more dishwashing for us, more hired help in the house.

"Measles, mumps, whooping cough and other children's diseases were experienced by us all. These diseases were not so serious as a fever that laid me low. It soon went to my head and made me unconscious for days.

Dr. Bowman: "It looks like brain fever."

Mother: "So it's dangerous?"

Dr. Bowman: "It is very serious."

The Doctor made daily visits with little hope of my recovery, but Mother said, "it couldn't be, he must get well." They stood around the bed, the Doctor watching closely for any signs of life other than the respiration, when the Doctor whispered, "did you see the twitching of the muscles of the big toe on the right foot?" The movement of the toes was the first sympton of returning life.

"The receipt of a letter in our household was an

event. The relatives in Michigan were cut off when we came west. Seldom did letters pass so when Father brought a letter from the village post office addressed to Mother, we all were excited standing on tiptoe to hear the news. "Well," she said, "Grandpa and Sarah are coming to visit us!" We jumped up and down, ran around the house and jumped over the barricade at the door to keep the baby from getting out. "When are they coming?" "Where shall we meet them?" and many other questions were proposed. At last the great day arrived. We all went in the lumber wagon to meet them in Rock Island. Grandpa Forbush was now a gray haired man with gray whiskers, a short man, a hard worker, a pioneer, a successful farmer. Grandma Sarah was a young woman—Mother's step-mother. They brought a budget of news. Levanche and Elisha had settled on a farm in West Bloomfield and have a baby, Edwin; Henry and his family were making a good living in Pleasant Valley; Cordon was crippled and couldn't work; your baby brother, Ed, has married and settled on a farm about three miles east of Pontiac; Frank Orr and Mack Bachelor would be better off if they would go to Pontiac less frequently; Van Hosner married Zeke Dye's daughter and lives in Commerce township about three miles Northeast of Walled Lake on the Pontiac road. Chalkley was doing well on the Eldad Smith place. Father and Mother lived their early lives over again and were eager to return to Michigan and visit all the relatives and friends. When we were tramping the fields next day and father told what he had accomplished on the farm, Grandpa turned to him and spoke in earnest tones: "Charles, you never can stand it to work as you do. What would happen if you should get sick?" Sarah said the same thing to Mother, but Mother replied: "What can a feller do, with a family of five children to clothe and feed and no money to hire help . . . . Butter at 20c, eggs at 10c won't buy many groceries these days."

"In the fall, 1873, Father met the third national financial panic which worked havoc with all farmers, falling heaviest upon farmers who carried mortgages on their lands and chattels. The years immediately following the close of the Civil War had seen a tremendous expansion of production, particularly of the staple crops. The demobilization of the armies released thousands of men for the farm and decreased the large demand for farm products for the army. War industries were closed, immigration increased, new farms were homesteaded, others were occupied and developed by the advance of settlers westward. Consequently, crop acreage and production increased amazingly and in consequence prices of wheat, corn, potatoes, pork, beef, and dropped in accordance with the law of supply and demand. Farmers found it difficult to make a living. They bought supplies and farm implements on credit and mortgaged their crops for payment at rates of interest that ate up the profits. Manufacturers were helped by the tariff, the farmers had to sell in competition with foreign products imported. The panic brought on by this condition and by speculations is said to have been "The greatest panic" in the history of the nation. The falling price of wheat spelled disaster to tens of thousands of farmers. From Father's account book, I have copied some of the items with prices, with which he paid John Templeton for work. These indicate the level of prices of farm products in this year: Corn was 25c a bushel, eggs 10c a dozen, butter 10c a pound, potatoes 25c a bushel, lard 8c a pound. Wheat was 90c a bushel.

"Father supplemented the proceeds of the farm with his earnings, in digging wells, laying up stone walls, making cisterns, in the harvest field. Even then in 1873 he and the boys dressed in cotton shirts and denim trousers and Louisa and Clara in calico. The furniture was reduced to the barest necessities. The food was pork, potatoes, corn meal and bread, milk and butter and crust coffee. The family was pinched by poverty in the winter of 1873-74.

"In the spring of 1874 when we were planting potatoes on the creek bottom land, Father was taken suddenly sick with pains and cramps that doubled him like a jackknife. Arthur and I were scared. We rolled him onto the stone boat and took him to the house, got him on the bed and went for Dr. Bowman who examined him and observed him a few minutes and said, "A very sick man." He came again in the evening, then early next morning and pronounced it "Cholera Morbus." "His physical condition is weak from overwork. His resistance is low. We will hope for the best."

CHAPTER XII

VILLAGE LIFE—WALLED LAKE

The residents of Walled Lake village welcomed Charles L. and his family. Twenty years had gone by since he left the Severance homestead and had made frequent visits to the village store and post office. Even so, he was known by the older residents such as Dr. Hoyt who had been the family physician in his father's family. Then, too, his brother, John, had lived in Walled Lake for six years. When Charles L. left St. Johns, his brother was a farmer in the neighborhood. John had suffered a serious accident. Many bones were broken when his team ran away while he stood on the wagon tongue between the horses, trying to repair a harness strap. He was picked up for dead. After lying several months in a cast waiting for the bones to heal, he recovered sufficiently to get about on crutches, but discovered that his left leg was three inches shorter than the right one. He was, therefore, incapacitated for heavy work of any kind. He learned his father's trade—cobbler and bootmaker—which his father had not practiced for thirty-five years. He settled in the village and erected a small shop just west of the Pennell Blacksmith Shop and repaired the boots of the boys and girls, and the men and women of the village and frequently made boots for the men. In this village of three hundred people and as many more in the countryside, he made a sufficient wage to support a family of eight.

He said to Charles L., who had spent the winter with his family at his father's homestead: "Better start a meat market in the village. The town is growing. There is only one vacant house—the one you are to purchase, next to mine on South Main St., owned by T. Welfare. There are five hundred people to be served from this point. There are two stores selling groceries and merchandise and other supplies, two blacksmith shops, a saw mill and a grist mill, which are patronized by farmers living from three to five miles away. There are two churches, well attended, and a good school for the children, no one selling meat nearer than Farmington, nine miles away. Novi and Wixom could be reached with the meat wagon. Here is your opportunity, with your growing boys to help you, you should make a good living."

The proposition appealed to Charles L. and the boys. He had many misgivings about his success in this industry owing to the condition of his health. He was a different man than he was twenty years ago when he left his father's farm. Time had dealt roughly with him. His "face was deeply furrowed as if by the marks of a ruthless hand, his whole figure seemed fearfully ravaged and broken, like a great forest maple shattered by the storm." The boy of fine physique and square shoulders was a man of forty-three now, with breast caved in and shoulders rounded. He had an intermittent cough and suffered at times with extreme cases of asthma which required him to sit up all night and breathe the fumes of burning salt peter or the smoke of stramonium leaves for relief. He started out with a stout heart, high hopes, and ideals, and with courage. He returned baffled, out done, broken in spirit, broken in body, hopes of a fine farm with well-tilled acres, good buildings, well-bred horses, and cows and hogs and sheep, vanished.

There is a worthy saying: "You can't keep a good man down." Charles was in the slough of despondency for a time, but he soon began to rally and to readjust himself to his new opportunities and environment. A profound economic change was taking place in the country, the change from agriculture to industry which he did not appreciate. His case was only one in a thousand where men were quitting the farm for the factory, for the mill, and for merchandising. John had said: "Meat market." Charles was thinking: "Meat market." He recalled his experience at hog killing time. He knew how to stick a hog and cut an artery with certain aim; how to dress a sheep and get the skin off, so the flesh would not taste of the wool; how to kill and dress beef cattle and the sure strike in the forehead that brought the steer to its knees. He said to Louisa: "Arthur is strong enough and courageous enough to bring a steer from the country to the slaughter-house which I could erect back by the woods. He could help dress the beef and the hogs.

MICHIGAN TRAILMAKERS 137

We could open a little market in the front yard next to the road which I could care for while Arthur is peddling meat among the farmers." So his hopes rose and the boys became assets to the family income just as they did when he was a boy working at home and just as the boys did in New Hampshire when his father worked for a neighbor and gave the earnings to the family expense fund. So Charles made another new start, this time in business. He became a butcher and Walled Lake and community acquired a meat market where its citizens might secure a variety of fresh meat according to their tastes.

"A spring wagon and a horse, butcher's tools, saws, knives, and meat block, and a building for a market and a slaughter-house were necessary in order to start business," he told John.

John asked: "Didn't you save money in Illinois?"

Charles: "No; too much sickness, too many bad years, prices too low. The fact is, the home was mortgaged for $1000 when I bought it. It was mortgaged for $1250 when I left. I made a poor living. I set out a ten acre orchard, just ready to bear, built an addition to the house, built a barn, broke up forty acres of wild land and put it under cultivation. I sold the farm for only $100 above the mortgage. I have some money which was realized from the sale of my stock and implements and machinery. I will have to borrow enough to pay for my horse and spring wagon. Mr. Moore who runs the saw mill will let me have lumber 'on time'."

In the southeastern corner of the yard of his home

facing the road and the lake was the little meat shop, a building about ten by twelve. It was equipped around the inside of the room with large hooks on which a whole beef or a hog or a sheep or a calf could be hung. In the center was the great wooden meat block. Near at hand were special knives, the long straight steel knife for cutting steaks, a short rounded blade for skinning animals, and a medium straight pointed steel blade for sticking hogs. There were meat saws, the cleaver, the scales, and the like. The meat in warm weather was kept in a cooler, just back of the shop—an underground room, covered with a gable roof resting on the ground on either side. The summer supply of ice was kept here under sawdust. The slaughterhouse was back across the muck swamp so that the stench would not reach the houses.

By seven o'clock in the morning, the Van Hosners living three miles out would hear the clang of a hand bell and the rumble of a spring wagon. Mrs. Hosner would rush to the door to meet a sixteen-year-old boy just driving his reddish brown mules and spring wagon up to the back door. She wanted a round steak. He got down, went to the back end of the wagon, opened the double doors of the big box and behold! a miniature meat shop with porterhouse, sirloin, and round steaks hanging on the hooks, hearts, tongues, rib roasts, spare ribs lying on the bottom! There were saws, knives, and steelyards for weighing. She may have purchased a ten pound roast for fifty cents or a five pound steak for a half dollar. Then he went on to his Uncle

Chalkley's and to his grandfather's and on around the circuit reaching home about three o'clock in the afternoon. The next day, Arthur covered a different section of the countryside. The family lived on the meat left over which would have otherwise spoiled. He "corned" cuts of beef not sold when fresh, salted down pieces of pork, not used immediately. Sausage, pressed beef, and bolognas were on sale. The village and the countryside were unable to consume enough meat to make the business a paying one, but it furnished a living for the family for four years and more. In the meantime, considerable building was in progress, masons were needed for laying the stone foundations, for building chimneys and for plastering at wages ranging from $2.00 to $2.50 a day, and even more if the work was done by the job and if the mason should work overtime. So it turned out that Arthur married and became an apprentice to his father in the mason trade. The market was abandoned or sold out. Arthur soon became the best and most reliable mason in this part of the country. Eugene, the second son, hired out to work by the month to Van Hosner. Palmer, the third son, became a "tender" for Arthur and soon learned the trade. The masons were known by their clothes when they came into the village after a day's work dressed in overalls spotted with white lime. Stone work was figured by the perch, plastering by the yard, chimney construction by the hundred brick.

Charles preferred to work by the job, so he could favor himself as he was unable to do a full day's work. This arrangement gave Arthur a chance to do apprentice work. Residents of Novi and Wixom, Orchard Lake, Straits Lake, and other places equally distant sent for the Severance boys to do their work. Spreading plaster and laying field stone which had to be broken with a ten-pound hammer and trimmed, and then lifted onto the wall was too strenuous for Charles. He was physically unable to stand the work.

In the spring, if there were no jobs of masonry ready the boys turned their hands to sheep shearing, an art which they learned from their father who worked with them. They sheared twenty-five or thirty sheep a day at seven cents apiece. In the winter they hauled and cut up a year's supply of stove wood.

After finishing with the meat market, he conceived the idea of buying eggs, poultry, butter, veal calves, lambs from the farmers and of taking them to Detroit to market. With his experience in purchasing for the meat market and in estimating the weight of hogs, calves and lambs, he could go through the countryside and buy up a crate of chickens, a calf, a pig, a lamb, a few crates of eggs and have a load every week or two. He would start from the Lake about four o'clock in the morning and drive over the plank road to Novi and over the Grand River turnpike through Farmington to the six-mile house before dark. Up early the next morning, he would get his load on the Detroit market by six o'clock in the morning in time for the early buyers. Then he would drive late into the night on the return trip and reach home on the next day. At least three days were required for the trip. The second year of huckstering was the better; the turnover was larger. He concluded that he would make more money by shipping his goods by freight to a commission merchant in Buffalo. He opened negotiations with one and finally shipped him a consignment of meats and apples worth more than $100 with freight prepaid. The shipment reached its destination, then the firm evidently vanished. He could not get the money and he could not find the firm. His frequent losses consumed his profits. He concluded that he would be as far ahead at the end of the year if he spent more time swapping stories with the "never sweats" who congregated daily in John's shoe shop or in Gage's grocery, but neither one would furnish bread for his family. The long tedious day and night rides were so exhausting that Charles was compelled to discontinue.

Masonry and sheep shearing were not all the year round jobs, so Charles found other work to piece out. Then, too, there was more building in some years than in others. Once he rented a twenty-acre lot from John Dolbear so the boys would have something to do and planted it to potatoes. At another time, he worked forty acres of the old homestead about two and one-half miles distant. Later still he rented the Compton farm about one and one-half miles west of the village, but he continued with Palmer's assistance to work at masonry. Between farming and masonry, the whole family kept busy. Charles was a farmer who did not believe in putting all his eggs in one basket. He raised corn, oats, cucumbers, built houses and barns, sheared sheep so that if one activity failed, another would furnish a living.

II

Charles wanted his children to have ampler opportunities for an education than he had enjoyed. It was not possible to keep the boys in school in Andalusia because of the work on the farm and the distance Arthur and Eugene must go to school. While he lived at Walled Lake, his children had all the advantages that other children of the village enjoyed. They were never kept from school for work. The village school had the reputation of being the best of its kind in the country. None of the districts could boast of better teachers than Sadie Bicking, Riley Keith, Frank Erwin, and others who taught the village school. Charles had acquired the rudiments of a district school education in the Green District which were supplemented by practical experience. He had many occasions to use and to increase his knowledge of arithmetic in his business. He acquired a taste for reading. There were few books in his home but there was always a newspaper and the almanac. He read all the books he could get. He once received a set of T. B. Macaulay's History of England with his subscription to the Detroit Free Press and read it with delight and passed it on to his boys. He would read the boys' text books on history and would help solve their arithmetic problems without touching pencil to the slate. He encouraged Eugene, Henry, and Clara, who wanted to teach school, to enter the Normal College at Ypsilanti. He did not know one note from another nor the difference between a sharp and a flat, but he insisted on his children's attending a four-weeks' "Singing School" conducted in the church by Palmer Hartsough.

III

In a trial in the court house in Springfield, an attorney asked the witness from New Salem where Lincoln once lived: "Who are the leading men of New Salem?"

Witness replied: "We have no leading men. They are all leading men." So it was in this village of Walled Lake. Charles was on good terms with them all. His credit was good at the stores for a year's supply of groceries, if he had wanted so much credit. He often "swapped stories" and gossiped and talked politics with the men who frequented John's Shoe Shop and Gage's Store.

He was a member of the "Gun Club", members of which practiced shooting with the rifle and the shot gun. The Club held shooting matches Friday afternoons in J. J. Moore's pasture. Live pigeons were used at first. The pigeon was placed in a spring trap which at the signal was sprung throwing the pigeon fifteen or twenty feet into the air. The marksman took aim and shot just as the pigeon opened his wings to fly. Sympathy for the wounded birds was so great that the Club voted to substitute globular glass shells for birds. The globular shells, the size of baseballs, were thrown into the air by means of a spring trap. The marksman would fire when and after the shell reached its maximum height.

Charles probably received his greatest thrills out of fishing. He once caught an eight-pound pickerel and the possibility of catching another kept his interest and spirits up. He would sit in an old flat boat all the afternoon, waiting for a bite and get nothing but a nibble, but more often he caught a mess of perch, sunfish, and roach. At other times, he would still fish with minnows either early in the morning or late in the afternoon when the family might expect a rock bass, or a black bass. At other times, when a gentle breeze ruffled the water, he would troll around the lake, and frequently get a black bass and occasionally a pickerel. When he left his baited hooks at the dock, he might expect to get a bullhead the next morning.

During the fall months, he went spearing at night. A torch light in the bow of the boat shed enough light into the water so the spearmen, standing and searching the shallow bottom on either side of the boat, could see the fish lying on the bottom. Then, if his aim was good and if he could make allowance for the refraction of light on the surface of the water, he could spear his fish. It required one man or boy to sit on the back seat and paddle the boat along quietly. Two hours of fun and work would result in enough fish for two or three families.

In the winter time, he cut holes through the ice and let down a baited hook. Later he pushed out on the ice a little frame house two by three feet and placed it over a hole in the ice three or four inches in diameter. When a bass or a pickerel stuck his nose up the hole for air, Charles would get him with the spear.

Charles was not a betting man, although he did bet and win a felt hat on the election of Garfield to the presidency of the United States. He had learned from his experience with the knitting machine not to take chances. He built many "aircastles" out of his fertile imagination, but when the question of making a small investment in a "get rich quick" scheme was asked, he would say: "You can't get something for nothing." During the mild winter weather, a layer of ice one and one-half to two feet thick covered the lake. Saturday afternoons were the holidays or playtime for the community. The boys and girls were on their skates, others on their sleds pushed or drawn by skaters, others slid on the smooth ice. A crowd would assemble about a hundred feet from the shore by the village for visits and games. Many horses and cutters were there. If a man thought his horse had any speed, he would race him across to the point and back, about a half mile each way. Clark Jones was sure to appear with his little bay mare and out distance any trotter on the ice. The crowd cheered as he made the home base. Hank Hodge of West Bloomfield was in town on one of these occasions. He drove his speckled Arabian horse with ill-fitting harness and a home-made cutter onto the ice. After limbering up the horse by driving him back and forth a few times, he found himself starting across with his old horse abreast of Jones' little mare. He drew the lines taut and yelled "Go". His old horse took the bit in his teeth, leaped forward, kept the lead and made the goal a rod ahead of Jones' bay mare. Shouts and applause arose from the good natured crowd, wagers were not made, wagers were not paid. Would anyone have bet on the old horse! At any rate, all the racing here was for pleasure, not for profit.

IV

Charles took his religion with moderation as he did his politics. He was not radical, nor was he extremely conservative. He was brought up in the church and knew the doctrines and teachings as they were expounded by the preachers of his day. He was baptised in the Mississippi River and united with the Baptist Church of Andalusia and subsequently transferred his membership to the Walled Lake Baptist Church where it remained until his death. His whole family, John and Chalkley and their families were members here, too. He lived through the period of sensation caused by the lectures of Robert G. Ingersoll on the mistakes of Moses and the beginnings of the controversy started by Bible students who applied scientific principles to the study of the Bible, who were execrated at the time and called "higher critics". While Charles' faith was not greatly disturbed by these new ideas, yet he was led to question some of the current beliefs of the church that the Bible was verbally inspired; that Adam was the first man to live on the earth when history recorded a Chinese civilization before Adam's time; and that Jehovah drowned all the peoples and every living thing on the earth except Noah's household in the Ark, and the like. His mind was open to new ideas. He held to the essentials of religion and had a strong abiding faith in the spiritual values of life as contrasted with material values.

In early life, he worked to the limit of his strength and of his endurance with the hope of acquiring a farm free of debt and some luxuries in later life. Then, he was stricken with illness and lost practically all he had gained. He was an old man at forty and was never able, thereafter, to do a full hard day's work, with few exceptions. He readjusted himself to his new problems and conditions and took life more moderately. His chief desire for his boys was that they grow to be honest, useful, prosperous men with high ideals of life, with loyalty to home, to church, to state. From this time on the boys largely directed the activities of the home and earned the money to support the family. The father's incapacity gave responsibility and initiative to the boys. The mother and daughter, Clara, also assisted by keeping boarders at the time of the construction of the Air Line of the Grand Trunk railway from Walled Lake to Wixom. The greatest service he rendered the boys was to give them the opportunity to help themselves.

He was unselfish in many ways. He would inconvenience himself to accommodate a friend. He purchased a new mower, and against the protests of his sons loaned it to farmer Jim for cutting ten acres of grass. Tramps came to his door after the railroad was finished and while he lived near it on the Compton farm and they were always fed. He went so far as to keep some of them overnight.

"Never go to law," was Charles' advice to his boys. This was given after a sad experience in the Probate Court of Oakland County. After his mother, Martha, died, Elmina kept house for her father until she married Frank Sherman. Then Jotham married and lived on the home place and cared for his father. Finally, his father went to Chalkley's to live. He gave Chalkley a legal document, a power of attorney, so that he could care for all the business interests of his father, and later he made a will, properly witnessed, bequeathing all his property to Chalkley.

Chalkley, who had farmed the Eldad Smith place for twenty years, was a prosperous farmer. His farm was well stocked, his teams of horses and mules were ample. His hired men were five or six at a time in addition to his sons. He drove a three-seated spring wagon in which he brought his family of eight to church at Walled Lake. He was a deacon in the Baptist Church in which John and Charles were members. His eldest son, Thomas Chalkley, was in the high school at Pontiac preparatory to entering the university. He was an officer in the Grange and altogether a prominent man in the county. At this juncture the father died and the will which bequeathed all his property to Chalkley was entered for probate with Thomas L. Patterson,

Judge of Probate of Oakland County. Nathan, Charles, and John felt that they should have received a portion of the property inasmuch as they helped to earn the property, and that their father was unduly influenced to give his fine home and farm to the son who already possessed as good a farm. Accordingly, they contested the will. James D. Bateman of Walled Lake represented the brothers; Arthur L. Tripp of Pontiac was Attorney for Chalkley. Several months were required for taking testimony. The expenses mounted on either side. Mr. Bateman must be paid from time to time, so must Mr. Tripp. Money was required for witness fees. Nathan furnished part, Charles furnished some—money that the boys had earned and put into the family treasury. Later the best horse on the farm, named Duck, of which Eugene was very fond and often drove in front of the carriage when he went to house parties and to church, was sold to help meet the expenses of the suit. Charles was optimistic until the decision was rendered by the Judge. He said: "I know we will win," and staked more money on the game like a gambler at his cards. The Judge upheld the will.

Twenty years passed. Charles visited Chalkley on a small farm near South Lyon. He was living alone, got his own meals and ate them alone, made his own bed, did all the chores, planted and harvested the corn, dug the potatoes, everything alone. A lonely man, on a lonely farm, on a lonely road. His wife, Martha McCall, died while the suit over the will was in progress. The Eldad Smith place where the two brothers began life in partnership was sold on account of the mortgage. The father's home to which he moved from the Smith place, and around which clung many pleasant memories of his and of his sisters and brothers was sold to satisfy creditors. The big white house and barns were burned to the ground and the big farm which these intrepid pioneers had purchased and improved had passed out of the possession of the Severances. Chalkley's eldest daughter, Martha, went insane shortly after the family moved to the homestead; Thomas C., a graduate of the university, died of typhoid fever; Howard, the youngest son, was instantly killed by a bolt of lightning, and Mabel, the baby of the family, who grew to womanhood without a mother's care, and became a teacher of home economics, and died. The brothers renewed their friendship although it was cold and distant. There was a cordial feeling between the boys of the several families. No antipathy developed.

When the estate of Edwin Forbush was finally settled, a few acres of the homestead was inherited by Louisa. Charles purchased her brother Cordon's share of the inheritance and, with Arthur's help, erected a house and barn on the little farm. From the east door of the house, Charles and Louisa could see the old home and the large maple tree under whose branches they were married forty years before. They were Grandpa and Grandma now. They travelled the periphery of the circle which began at Straits Lake and ended there, covering the intermediate points of the Eldad Smith farm, the home in St. Johns, the struggle for existence on the Andalusia farm and the new start in the village of Walled Lake. Like "the rolling stone that gathers no moss" they returned to the home base nearly empty handed as far as material wealth is concerned. The years had brought them rich experience and character development and a deep appreciation of the spiritual values of life. They were keenly interested in their children and the development of their families in which they found their greatest pleasure. Here was their wealth.

The reunion of the family in 1899 at Straits Lake was one of the happiest occasions of their lives. Their sons and daughter and their in-laws and children were all home with one exception. It was a mild August day when light breezes from the lake played among the foliage and frolicked around the children and the older folk as they sat or played in the shade of the oaks and maples in the front yard. Arthur and Linda, with their little flock, came the day before from South Lyon, fifteen miles away. Arthur was a master mason and had worked with his father at the trade many years. He and Linda were extremely unselfish; always loyal and devoted to their parents. Grandpa and Grandma loved their children, Stephen, Adah, Ora, Margaret, and all the other grandchildren. Eugene, a Baptist minister, holding a pastorate at Reading, was unable to be present. He was graduated from the Michigan Normal School and had a year's work in the Law School of the University. A message of cheer and solicitation was sent by the family to him and

Frances and baby Evelyn. Palmer and Mary came too with their robust tribe of children—Willie, Elmer, Madgie, Grace, and Henry. Palmer was a mason, too; also a farmer. Henry and Anna drove in from Ann Arbor. He, too, enjoyed the advantages of the Michigan Normal School, then officiated as Superintendent of Schools in Lakeview and now, after earning the M. A. degree at the University of Michigan, was an Assistant in the University Library. Clara Weatherhead came early with her husband, Albert. She, too, was trained in the Normal School and had taught in the District school. Charles Junior, the youngest of the family, lived at home. He, too, was a school teacher and a farmer.

The men constructed a temporary table in the shade in the front yard. Clara, Linda and Mary, a very efficient combination, piled the table high with potatoes, chicken, bread and other good things to eat. There were twenty-one at the table. After the children left the table for play, the older folk lingered at the table with Grandpa and Grandma and passed the afternoon in reminiscences, jokes, stories, gossip and in conversation on the intimate and serious things of their lives.

Within the next decade these Michigan pioneers finished their work and with clean records, passed on. The thought is expressed in the words of Kitty McCoy, the Oakland County poetess:

> "But faithfully they toiled away,
> And at the closing of life's day
> Had won the praise the faithful claim
> With the glory of an honest name."

BIBLIOGRAPHY

Adams, Romanzo. Agriculture in Michigan. (Mich. Pol. Sci. Ass'n, v. 3, pp. 163-202.)

Barber, Edward W. Recollections and Lessons of Pioneer Boyhood. (In Mich. P. & H. Collection, v. 31, p. 178.)

Beal, W. J. Pioneer Life in Southern Michigan in the Thirties. (In Mich. P. & H. Collection, v. 32, p. 236.)

Catlin, George B. The Story of Detroit. Detroit, Detroit News, 1923.

Chase, Supply. A Pioneer Minister. (In Mich. P. & H. Collection, v. 4, page 52.)

Cooley, Thomas M. Michigan. Boston, Houghton, 1890.

Copley, A. B. The Pottawattomies, (In Mich. P. & H. Collection, v. 14, p. 256.)

Crawford, C. C. Reminiscences of Pioneer Life in Michigan. (In Mich. P. & H. Collection, v. 4, p. 41.)

Cutcheon, Byron M. Fifty years of Growth in Michigan. (In Mich. P. & H. Collection, v. 22, p. 479.)

Drake, Thomas J. History of Oakland County. (In Mich. P. & H. Collection, v. 3, p. 559; v. 22, p. 408.)

Durant, Samuel W. & H. B. Pierce. History of Oakland County, Michigan with Illustrations, descriptive of its scenery, palatial residences, etc. Phila. L. H. Everets & Co., 1877.

Fuller, George Newman. Economic and Social Beginnings of Michigan. Lansing, Michigan; State Printers, 1916.

Garland, Hamlin. A Son of the Middle Border. New York, Macmillan, 1917.

Garland, Hamlin. Trailmakers of the middle Border. New York, Macmillan, 1926.

Glidden, A. C. Pioneer Farming. (In Mich. P. & H. Collection, v. 18, p. 418.)

Hale, Philip Henry ed. Hale's History of Agriculture by Dates. ed. 5. St. Louis. Hale Publishing Company, 1915.

Hoyt, James M. History of the Town of Commerce. (In Mich. P. & H. Collection, v. 14, 1889.)

Joy, James F. Railroad History of Michigan. (In Mich. P. & H. Collection, v. 22, p. 292.)

Lamb, Caleb A. Incidents in Pioneer Life, (v. 1, p. 149.) Reminiscences. (Mich. P. & H. Collection, v. 5, p. 47.)

McClintock, Walter. The Old North Trail; or Life Legends and Religion of the Black Feet Indians. London, Macmillan, 1910.

McLaughlin, Andrew C. Lewis Cass. Boston, Houghton, 1891.

Mathews, Lois K. The Expansion of New England. Boston, Houghton, 1909.

Nevins, Allan. The Emergence of Modern America, 1865-1878. New York, Macmillan, 1927. (Hist. of Am. Life, v. 8.)

Norton, Henry K. The Story of California. Chicago, McClurg, 1913.

Norton, John M. A Picture of Memory-Settlement of Oakland County. (In Mich. P. & H. Collection, v. 22, p. 404.)

Nowlin, William. The Bark-Covered House or Pioneer Life in Michigan. (In Mich. P. & H. Collection, v. 4, p. 480.)

Parkins, Almon E. The Historical Geography of Detroit. Lansing, Michigan Historical Commission, 1918.

Parrish, Randall. Historic Illinois; The Romance of the Earlier Days. Chicago, McClurg, 1905.

Poppleton, O. Early History of Oakland County. (In Mich. P. & H. Collection, v. 17, p. 556.)

Randall, C. D. The Pottawattomies. (In Mich. P. & H. Collection, v. 7, p. 149.)

Sanford, Albert H. The Story of Agriculture in the United States. Boston, Heath, 1916.

Soper, Sarah E. Reminiscences of Pioneer Life in Oakland County 1824-1860. (In Mich. P. & H. Collection, v. 28, p. 399.)

Tiffin, Edward. Surveyor-General. Report on the Survey of Michigan Lands. November 30, 1815. (In Mich. P. & H. Collection, v. 18, p. 661.)

True, Alfred C. A History of Agricultural Education in the United States 1785-1925. (U. S. Dept. of Ag. Misc. Pub. 36, 1929.)

U. S. Bureau of American Ethnology. Bulletin 30. Handbook of American Indians North of Mexico. 2 vols. Washington, 1907.

Utley, Henry M. Michigan as a Province territory and State; The 26th member of the Federal Union by Henry M. Utley and Byron M. Cutcheon. 4. v., 1906. Publishing Society of Michigan. 1906.

Utley, H. M. The Wild Cat Banking System of Michigan. (In Mich. P. & H. Collection, v. 5, p. 209.)

Van Buren, A. D. P. The Fever and Ague—"Michigan Rash—Mosquitoes—the old Pioneer's Foes." (In Mich. P. & H. Collection, v. 5, p. 300.)

Van Buren, A. D. P. "Raisings" and "Bees" Among the Early Settlers. (In Mich. P. & H. Collection, v. 5, p. 296.)

Van Buren, A. D. P. The Log School House era in Michigan. (In Mich. P. & H. Collection, v. 14, p. 283.)

Van Buren, A. D. P. What the Pioneers ate and How They Fared. Michigan Food and Cookery in the Early Days. (In Mich. P. & H. Collection, v. 5, p. 293.)

Van Buren, A. D. P. The Frolics of Forty-five Years Ago. Some of the Social Amusements of the early Settlers. (In Mich. P. & H. Collection, v. 5, p. 304.)

Watkins, L. D. The Old Log House (illus.) (In Mich. P. & H. Collection, v. 26, p. 644.)

INDEX

Agriculture Expansion, western prairies, 132; Illinois, 114 et seq. Michigan, 40 et seq; 62, et seq; 93; 99-101; 109; 149. New York, 6; 11.
Algonquin tribe of Indians, 47;
Albany, 9, 11.
Allan, Ed. 72.
Almanac, 69; 70.
Andalusia, Ill., 114 et seq; 150.
Andalusia Creek, 115, 116.
Andrews, John, 68, 73, 86, 88.
Ann Arbor, 93, 152.
Apples—varieties, 60.
Avon, Oak. Co., 7.

Bachelder, Abbey. 72.
Bachelor, Consider. 68, 72.
Bachelor, Mack. 75, 86-89.
Bachelor, Samuel. 72, 73, 92.
Bachelor, Sidney. 72.
Bachelor Settlement, 74, 82, 95.
Bangs, Joshua. 14.
Bank of Kensington, 52.
Bank of Sandstone, 52.
Banks and banking, 52.
Baptist Church — Andalusia, 124.
Baptist Church — Farmington, 24.
Baptist Church—Pontiac, 71.
Baptist Church—West Farmington, 40, 41, 71.
Baptist Church—Walled Lake, 47, 146.

Baptist Missionary Convention, New York, 2.
Barnum's Circus, 127.
Bateman, James D., 149.
Bee trees, 60.
Berry, Sam 14.
Bennets' Point, 80.
Bible. 69.
Bicking, Sadie, 142.
Binding wheat, 63.
Birmingham, 72, 73, 93.
Black Hawk, chief, 128.
Black Hawk War, 128.
Blackhawk Country, 116.
Bloomfield township, Oak. Co., 7.
Boat trip—New Haven to Chicago, 117.
Bois Blank, 17.
Bowman, Dr. 125, 130.
Boy's earnings, 58; boy's life in Mich., 58 et seq; boy's life in N. E. 5, 6.
Boy's work on the farm, 126.
Breaking new ground, 48.
Brindle cow, 129.
Buckwheat, 49.
Buffalo, New York, 7; 9; 12; 13.

California, 78.
Canal boats, 10.
Canada, 17, 19.
Canandaigua, New York, 19.
Capital of Michigan, Detroit; 20.

INDEX

Caravans to California, 80.
Carson, General Kit, 78.
Cass, Lewis, 94.
Cattle, Durham, 94; Holstein, 94.
Chandler, Zach. 94.
Changing work—threshing, 84.
Chicago, 13, 21.
Chicago, Burlington & Quincy, 110.
Chicago & Northwestern, 110.
Chicago & Rock Island, 101, 110, 117.
Chicago turnpike, 14, 20.
Chilblains, 62.
Chimney building, 139.
China, history, 147.
Cholera Morbus, 133.
Chores, 45, 60.
Church. See names of churches.
Church in New England, 4.
Church services in the Hosner schoolhouse, 82.
Cider making, 60.
Circuit riders, 71, 74.
Civil War, 132.
Clarkson, Cayuga Co., New York, 73.
Clearing the land, 31, 38.
Clinton River, 21.
Clothes, weaving, 51.
Coe, John, 34.
Coe, William, 73.
Coldwater, 14, 20.
Commerce Circuit, 71.
Commerce—schooner, 7.
Commerce twp., 73.
Compton, Jacob. Farm, 141, 148.
Cooking utensils, 36.

Cord wood, 120.
Corduroy road, 21, 22.
Covered wagon, 9, 10, 12, 19, 28.
Covered wagon train, 78.
Crust coffee, 50.
Curing meat, 63.

Dearborn, 21.
Denver, Colo., 80.
Detroit, 1, 2, 7, 9, 14, 15, 17, 19, 20, 22, 29, 42, 82, 93.
Detroit Free Press, 47, 69, 142.
Detroit & Grand River Turnpike, 93.
Detroit & Milwaukee railway, 107.
Detroit & Pontiac road, 21.
Detroit & Pontiac railroad, 93.
Detroit & St. Joseph Railroad (Mich. Central) 93.
Detroit River, 17.
Devereaux, Seymour, 33, 101.
Disembarking at Detroit, 8.
"Dismal Swamp", 28.
District school, punishment, 69; boarding 'round, 69; spelling matches, 67-68.
Dodge, Betsey, 4.
Dodge, Harvey, 33.
Douglas, Stephen, 95.
Dye, Ezekiel, 33, 90, 101, 131.

Early settlers, 24, 65.
Education, 65, 69.
Emigrant song, 15.
English Reader (Murray) 67.
Erie Canal, 9, 10, 28.
Erie, Lake, 9, 12, 16.
Erwin, Frank, 142.
Express boats, 10.

INDEX

Family worship, 24.
Farm machinery, 108, 109.
Farm wages, (1867) 109.
Farmer, Elisha, 86, 131.
Farmer, Lavancha (Forbush) 75-77, 90, 91.
Farming—Illinois, 118-19.
Farming—Michigan, 94, 141.
Farming in war time, 108.
Farmington, 7, 22, 24, 74, 93.
Farmington twp. 25.
Fever and ague, 54.
Fireplaces, 35.
Fishing, 61, 96, 144.
Flint, 14, 21.
Flower seed, 39.
Following the trail, 12.
Food, 50, 90.
Forbush, Bliss, 73.
Forbush, Catherine, 72, 74.
Forbush, Cordon, 72, 73, 75, 76, 131.
Forbush, Edwin, 68, 72, 73, 74, 87, 90, 95, et seq., 131.
Forbush, Edwin, estate, 150.
Forbush, Edwin, Jr., 75, 76, 77, 84-86, 88.
Forbush, Henry, 75, 76, 79, 80, 92, 93, 131.
Forbush, Louisa, 68, 75-77, 89-91, 96, 98.
Forbush, Lyvonia, 72, 73.
Fort Bridger, 78.
Fort Wayne, 17.
Free Bank Act, 1837, 52.
Free Soilers, 94.
Furniture, 36.

Gage, Stephen, 141.
Games, see sports and games.
Genessee Co., N. Y. 3.
Geneva N. Y., 7, 12, 13, 28.

German mark, 53.
German settlements, 72.
Gilbert, Joseph, 7.
Gold dust, 80-81.
Gold in California, 78, 80.
Goode, Mr. 123.
Graham, John, 2.
Graham, Jonathan B., 14.
Grand River turnpike, 22, 28, 140.
Grand Trunk railway air line division, 147.
Greene, Aldis Emmet, 25, 34, 66.
Greene, William, 95.
Greene—School District, 66.
Grist mill, Farmington, 49, 60.
Gun club, Walled Lake, 143.

Hahnemann, 42.
Harger, Seeley, 73, 83, 87, 88, 92.
Harrison, William Henry, 47.
Hartsough, Christopher, 2.
Hartsough, Palmer, 143.
Hartsough, Sarah, 42.
Hartsough, Wells (Thankful) 12, 24, 25, 30, 41, 42, 51, 56.
Harvesting, 62, 119.
Haying, 62.
Hersey, John, 3.
Higher critics, 146.
Highway N. Y. to Mich., via Ohio, 12.
Hillsdale, 14, 21.
Hodge, Hank, 145.
Hog killing, 63.
Holly, 107.
Homesteads for soldiers of War, 1812, 1, 2.

INDEX

Homeopathic system of medicine, 43.
Honey, 51, 60.
Horses—Clydesdale & Percheron, 94.
Horse power tread mill, 83.
Horse racing on the ice, 145.
Hosner, Martin Van Buren, 72, 75, 88, 131.
Hosner, Thomas, 72.
Hosner School, 67, 73, 74.
Hosner School—Church services, 92.
House raisings, 34.
Household goods, 12.
Housekeeping, 76.
Housework, 50.
Houston, John, 116, 121, 124, 125.
Howell, 93.
Hoyt, Dr. James M. 55, 134.
Husking corn, 64.
Huckstering, 140.
Hymns, 16, 24.

Ice for summer, 123.
Illinois, 59.
Illinois farm, 114 et seq.
Immigration to Mich., 9, 21, 24, 25, 117.
Independence, Mo., 80.
Indian maidens, 45.
Indian ponies, 44.
Indians, 44; Indians—Walled Lake—26-27, 44.
Ingersoll, Robert G. 146.

Jackson, Andrew. 53.
Johns, Horace. 4, 7, 27, 28.
Johns, Thankful (Lamb) 28.
Jones, Clark 145.

Kansas, 13.
Kansas-Nebraska Bill, 94-95.
Keith, Riley 142.
King. See Prentice & King.
Knitting machine, 103, 106.

Lake steamers, 9.
Lakeview, Mich., 152.
Lamb, Caleb 3, 6, 7, 11, 23-25, 41, 42-43, 70; Physician, 102; St. Johns, 107-8.
Lamb, Isaac W. 99, 102-4, 106, 112.
Lamb, Martha, 4, 7.
Lamb, Nehemiah 3, 7, 13, 24, 71, 102.
Lamb, Roswell 3, 6, 102.
Lamb, Susan 6, 7, 12.
Land office—Detroit, 29.
Land speculators 20, 25, 29, 53.
Lands—sales—1831-1837, 1, 52; Land surveyor's report, 2.
Lansing, 22, 93.
Latch string, 35.
Lenox, N. Y., 11.
Lighting, 35, 51.
Lincoln, Abraham 95, 110-111, 128.
Line boats, 10.
Logging bees, 34, 48.
Log houses, 33, 34.
Log schoolhouse, 66.
Loom, 37.
Luther, Martin, Hymn, 16.

Macaulay, T. B., History of England, 142.
McCormick reaper, 62.
McCoy, Kitty, poem, 152.
Machinery, 94.
Mail carrier—Walled Lake & Farmington 46.

INDEX

Maine, 44.
Malden, Canada, 19.
Maple syrup, 51, 60.
Markets and marketing, 82, 93, 128, 140.
Martineau, Harriet, 21.
Masonry, 121, 139.
Meat market—Walled Lake—135-136, 138.
Melon patch, 126.
Methodist church, 71.
Methodist missionaries, 71.
Michigan Central railroad, 101.
Michigan Normal College, Ypsilanti, 151-152.
Michigan University, 151, 152.
Michigan soil, 11.
Michigan southern railroad, 101.
Michigan state college of Agriculture, 94.
Michigan—steamer, 13.
Mining gold, 80.
Missionaries in Oakland Co., 2, 3, 71.
Missionaries in Washtenaw Co., 3.
Missionaries in Wayne Co., 3; see also Baptist & Methodist churches.
Missouri Compromise, 94.
Mississippi River, 115.
Mohawk & Genessee turnpike, 9, 12.
Mohawk River, 9.
Morse, Samuel (Rev.), 97.
Mosquitoes, 55.
Mt. Clemens, 14, 21.
Murray, Theron, 25, 34, 56, 66.
Mush and milk, 51.

New England, 57, 65, 70, 73.
New England, Agriculture, 2, 6.
New England song, 15.
New York, 57.
New York Baptist Convention, 71, 102.
Niles, Mich., 27.
Northville, Mich., 7, 29, 30.
Novi, Mich., 4, 7, 22, 93, 135.
Norwegian settlements, 72.

Oakland Co., Mich., 1-3, 11.
Ontario Co., N. Y., 7.
Orchard Lake, 47, 72.
Oregon, 78.
Orr, Frank, 72, 75, 87, 92, 95, 107, 131.
Orr, William, 72.
Ottawa Indians, 47.
Overland mail, Farmington to Walled Lake, 46.
Over-production, 120, 132.
Owosso, 107.
Ox yokes, 60.

Packing houses, 110.
Palmer, F. J. T. firm, 19.
Palmer, Friend, 2, 19.
Palmer, Thomas, 2, 8, 13, 19-20.
Palmer, Thomas W., 20.
Palmer—a town—later called St. Clair, 20.
Panama, 78.
Panic, 1837, 53.
Panic, 1867, 102, 107.
Panic, 1873, 132.
Passenger coaches, 93.
Patterson, Thomas L., 148.
Paw Paw, Mich., 14.
Peddling meat, 138.

INDEX

Pens, 66.
Penn. oil fields, 110.
Phelps, 67, 68.
Phelps, William, 14.
Pine Lake, Oak. Co., 72.
Pioneer life, 12.
Pioneers, 2, 3, 4, 7, 53, 56, 59.
Plank roads, 93, 140.
Planting corn, potatoes, etc., 39.
Plymouth, Mich., 7, 42.
Politics, 94.
Pontiac, Mich., 7, 14, 21, 71, 82.
Pontiac (Chief), 17, 47.
Pontiac & Detroit highways, 93.
Pontiac Baptist Church, 71.
Pontiac high school, 148.
Pontiac, Walled Lake and Ann Arbor highway, 93, 95.
Potatoes—planting, 119.
Pottawottomies, 46, 47.
"Power", 86-87.
Protracted meetings, 4.
Prentice and King, 44, 45, 46.
Prices of produce, 120-121, 133.
"Promised land", 78.

Rail splitting, 61.
Railroads across N. Y., 9.
Railroads west of Miss. River, 110.
Rate bills, 56.
Redford, 24.
Religion, 70, 71, 125.
Republican party organized, 94-5.
Rifle shot, 59.
Rock Island, 116.
Rouge River, 21.

Royal Oak, Mich., 93.
Runaway team, 129-130.

Saginaw, Mich., 14, 21.
Saint Clair, Mich., 20.
Saint Johns, 7, 106, 107, 151.
Saline, Mich., 21.
Salt Lake City, 80.
San Francisco, 78, 80.
Sand Hill, 42.
Scandinavians in U. S., 110.
Schenectady, N. Y., 9, 11.
Schools, 67, 68.
Schools, N. E., 5.
Schools, Walled Lake, 142.
Schooners, 80.
Scots' settlement at Orchard Lake, 72.
Settlement Oakland Co., 1, 2, 56.
Severance, Adelia, 57, 108.
Severance, Arthur & family, 106, 137, 139, 140, 151.
Severance, Charles, 1, 4, 5, 6, 7, 11-12, 15, 23-25, 32, 47, 51, 54, 56-7, 71, 107.
Severance, Charles L., 11, 13, 16, 44, 56 et seq. 82, 86, 88, 91-3, 95-112, 147-151.
Severance, Charles Jr., 106.
Severance Clara, 129.
Severance, Daniel, 4, 6.
Severance, Elmina, 148.
Severance, Ezra, 4, 6, 7, 12, 13, 15, 25, 30, 41.
Severance, Henry, 106, 152.
Severance, Eugene and family, 106, 130, 151, 152.
Severance, Horace, 42.
Severance, Howard, 150.
Severance, John, 108, 134, 149.
Severance, Jotham, 57.

INDEX

Severance, Lewis, 11, 13, 16, 43, 44, 54, 58.
Severance, Mabel, 150.
Severance, Martha, 150.
Severance, Martha McCall, 149.
Severance, Nathan, 6, 57, 149.
Severance, Palmer and family, 106, 152.
Severance, Perry, 106.
Severance, Reuben, 6.
Severance, Thomas Chalkley, 30, 86, 88, 103-5, 107-8, 148.
Severance, Thomas Chalkley Jr., 148, 150.
Severans, John. Salisbury Mass., 4.
Shakes, 34.
Sheep — Hampshire, Shropshire, 94.
Sherman, Frank, 148.
Sheskone, Chief, 45, 46.
Sickness, 54-55.
Singing school, 143.
Slavery, 94-95.
Smith, Eldad, 33.
Smith, Eldad Farm, 99, 107, 149.
Smoke house, 63.
Snowbound, 62.
South Lyon, Mich., 150, 151.
Sowing wheat by hand, 48.
Specie circular of Pres. Jackson, 53.
Specie certificates, 52.
Spelling book, Webster's, 66.
Spelling down, 67-68.
Spinning, 51.
Spinning wheel, 37.
Sports and games, 5, 6, 7, 145.
Stage coaches, 9, 21.
Steamer on Lake Erie, 13.

Stilson, Alonzo, 61.
Stilson, Solomon, 34, 56.
Stock raising, 94, 125-6.
Stony Point Baptist Church, 71.
Storm on Lake Erie, 16.
Straits Lake (middle), 95, 96, 150, 151.
Strohmeier, Gus and Will, 122.
Swamp lands, 1, 2.
Swedish settlements, 72.
Swimming hole, 122.

Tallow candles, 51, 60.
Taxes, 56.
Tecumseh, Chief, 17, 47.
Templeton, John, 124.
Tenny, William, 46.
Threshing at the Forbushes, 83-89.
Threshing machines — tread mill—50.
Tifflin, Edward, Survey of Mich., Lands, 1, 2.
Tippecano, battle, 47.
Topanibee, Chief, 47.
Tramps, 148.
Trapping, 68.
Travel. Highway, 10; steamboats, 9, 10; canal boats, 10; covered wagon, 9, 10, 12, 19, 28; stage coaches, 9, 21.
Trees—varieties, 33.
Tripp, Arthur L., 149.
Troy, Mich., 71.
Tuttle, Jesse, 47.

Union Pacific Railway, 80, 110.

Village life, 134 et seq.
Voyage across Lake Erie, 13.

INDEX

W. C. T. U., 34.
Walled Lake, 7, 26, 44, 71, 134, 142, 144-5.
War, 1812. Soldier's Homesteads. Mich., 1, 2.
Washington, N. H., 4, 5, 11, 13.
Weatherhead, Albert, 129.
Weaving, 37.
Welfare, John, 26, 44, 56.
Well digging, 121, 126, 133.
West Bloomfield Twp., 25, 72-3.

Wheat—sowing, 48; harvesting, 49; threshing, 49; winnowing, 50.
Whigs, 95.
Wild cat banks, 53.
Williams, Glover, 108.
Winter in Mich., 1835-6, 21.
Wisconsin, 13, 59.
Wixon, Mich., 8, 21.

Ypsilanti, Mich., 21.

Zodiac signs, 70.